Widening Our Circle

Widening Our Circle

Wisdom for Young Women Facing the Challenges of Depression, Relationships, Eating Disorders, and Other Issues

Joan S. Mishra, M.Ed.

Authors Choice Press

San Jose New York Lincoln Shanghai

Widening Our Circle
Wisdom for Young Women Facing the Challenges of Depression,
Relationships, Eating Disorders, and Other Issues

Authors Choice Press
an imprint of iUniverse.com, Inc.

For information address:
iUniverse.com, Inc.
5220 S 16th, Ste. 200
Lincoln, NE 68512
www.iuniverse.com

ISBN: 0-595-17701-8

Printed in the United States of America

Dedicated to the love and joy that exists in

the hearts of all young women

Epigraph

A human being is part of the whole, called by us "Universe," a part limited in time and space. He experiences himself, his thoughts and feelings as something separate from the rest—a kind of optical delusion of his consciousness. This delusion is a kind of prison for us, restricting us to our personal desire and to affection for a few persons nearest to us. Our task must be to free ourselves from this prison by widening our circle of compassion to embrace all living creatures and the whole of nature in its beauty. Nobody is able to achieve this completely, but the striving for such achievement is in itself a part of the liberation and foundation for inner security.

—Albert Einstein to a rabbi whose teenage daughter needed comforting

Contents

Acknowledgements

I would like to offer special thanks to Jessica Mishra for her help in editing the book. Her many suggestions and insights brought new light to the writing in several areas. I am also deeply grateful for her way of sharing her experiences and those of her friends so openly. Knowing these young women has made my life so much richer.

Introduction

This book is designed to answer some of the questions you may be asking deep inside yourself. You may not have even put certain questions into words, but just have a longing to find a solution to whatever is bothering you. Young women face a variety of personal challenges today. I have become especially aware of their needs as a result of my relationship with my daughter, Jessica, who is twenty, her friends and my students at a junior college. And, of course, once *I* was a young woman in my twenties. Even though I lived in a different social climate in a lot of ways, I still battled with some of the same conflicts.

Many times when Jessica talked to me about her friends' problems, I had the feeling that they were lacking some information. I felt if they simply knew some basic truths about life, they could find the happiness they were seeking. Naturally I had had many opportunities to discuss various subjects with my daughter over the years. It wasn't so easy to communicate these thoughts to her friends, because some ideas required a lot of time and energy in order to be absorbed. This is one reason I decided to write this book. It was a good means for me to talk to her friends and other young women in a more thorough and heartfelt way.

You or friends have probably battled with one or more of these issues: suicidal thoughts, depression, relationship struggles, eating disorders, or health problems. Although this seems like a wide-range of subjects, I believe the answers to these challenges all lie in the same fundamental truths. You can discover these truths for yourself by observing your own experience and by beginning to understand the thoughts of enlightened men and women, such as Einstein, Jesus, the Dalai Lama, Buddha, and other great teachers. Much of their guidance, I feel, will point you in this one direction—**the purpose of your life is to know your own inner Self.** You will be amazed to find that the closer you come to understanding *how* to do this, the closer you will come to being free from whatever problems weigh you down. It sounds so simple, and in a way, it is.

In order to make the information in this book as accessible as possible, I have divided it into many small sections marked by subtitles. I also have reviewed several of the concepts from different angles throughout the book as a way of helping the reader grasp the ideas more completely. Although I am directing the book at an audience of young women, say, ages 16 through 25, I feel it could also be valuable reading for parents who are looking for ways to help their daughters with adolescent issues. Hopefully, it will bring both parents and daughters a little closer to knowing the happiness and love inherent in their own higher Selves.

One

What is the Inner Self?

Of all the subjects discussed in this book this one ranks as the most essential. In fact, I believe this is the most important information you will ever learn about life. This is why I gave this point its own chapter. I wanted the information to really stand out in your mind. I will be discussing the inner Self throughout the book, so don't worry if you don't understand much about it yet. This chapter is just a first taste of the concept.

The Self goes by many different names in various religions and philosophies. Some people call it God. It is also known as the soul. When Buddha or a spiritual teacher talked about "realizing the Self", they meant that the person came to know the truth of their inner being. Such a realized being lives in a continuous state of love and joy. He or she is detached from anger, fear and other emotions. The person also feels a sense of unity with all things. Jesus, Buddha and many other saints and teachers have accomplished this goal. I believe it is the purpose of your life as well to move in that same direction. In fact, every life experience you have can bring you closer to understanding your own true Self.

The inner Self is not a place that only saints and great beings can contact. You feel its presence every day. When you feel affection as you look into a friend's eyes or hug your dog, you are experiencing the sensation of your own inner Self. When you get an impression of calm or simplicity walking in a forest, you are also sensing the nature of the Self. There are hundreds of other examples. Simply being aware of who you are, apart from your body, your thoughts and your feelings is also being aware of the Self.

Think back to when you were a very young child. Imagine being alive back then in that little body. Now notice how you feel in your present body. There is something that is *you* in both those bodies, even though those bodies are totally different. That sense of being you, of being alive and aware, is your true Self.

In yogic philosophy there is a Sanskrit word which beautifully describes the Self. The word is *satchitananda*. The three parts of the word describe different aspects of your inner Self. *Sat* means Truth. *Chit* refers to consciousness. And *ananda* represents bliss or happiness. In other words, the Self knows the nature of reality. The Self is also your own consciousness. It is your awareness of being here. And your Self lives in the constant condition of love and joy. Wouldn't it be amazing to live continuously in touch with this beautiful place that is right inside your own heart? When Jesus said, "The Kingdom of Heaven lies within," he was referring to the space of the Self. And in saying this, he was encouraging others to live in that same space he had realized. If you would like to read more about the nature of the Self, please see the resource section at that back of the book.

The opposite of living in continuous awareness of your inner Self is feeling depressed and suffering in some way. Suffering for young women today comes in many different forms: eating disorders, relationship problems with friends or parents, drug or alcohol addiction, sexual confusion, depression and thoughts of suicide. The hopeful news is that there is a message for you in every form of unhappiness you are experiencing. When you begin to understand what the universe is trying to communicate to you, you will become wiser and stronger, evolving to a higher level. It is my hope that this book will help you to unravel some of these messages.

There is a space in my heart for modern young women who are suffering in a deep way, because when I was a young adult, I went through several periods of anxiety and depression, and, at times, had thoughts of suicide. I was continually searching for answers on how to feel better. It took many years, but eventually I received most of the answers I needed from a variety of sources. For different reasons, I wasn't able to trust the wisdom of adults that were close to me, so I learned as best I could "on my own." Sadly, I feel many girls today are in the same position. I think it is very easy to become more lost when sources of truth and compassion seem absent.

I am so grateful for all that I have learned from studying books by spiritual masters, philosophers, psychologists, great writers and others. Their wise guidance along with learning from my own experience has brought me so much happiness. I no longer feel that I am alone, afraid, and disconnected from myself and others, as I did then. My deepest wish is that you will move in the same direction towards a sense of true freedom, and as Einstein said, widen your "circle of compassion to embrace all living creatures and the whole of nature in all its beauty."

Two

What is the Message behind Suicidal Feelings?

Of all the challenges young women face, the issue of suicide is the most painful and dramatic. You may have friends who have committed or attempted suicide, or you may have had thoughts of suicide yourself. Ophelia, a young woman in Shakespeare's play, *Hamlet*, suffered profound psychological distress and finally took her own life. She was unable to find any sources of love or comfort from the people she knew, although her father and brother continually poured advice on her. She found some temporary love from Hamlet, but he was as lost as she was, if not more. As you can see by this example, evidence that young women have been experiencing suicidal feelings exists even way back in the 1600's. If you are interested in this play, there is a recent version of it set in modern times that you can get on video.

In this chapter, I would like to share some thoughts I have on this subject that I hope will help you deal with these feelings in yourself or in friends.

How a Suicidal Person Feels

When you are very depressed, your mind is filled with negative thoughts. You may feel empty inside, as if you have no feelings. You may have anxiety, trouble breathing and a rapid heart beat. This is the body's way of expressing deep fear. If someone jumps out at you in a dark alley, you will have the same reaction. It is a very natural part of the range of feelings in a human being, so you needn't feel ashamed of it. If you get to

9

the point of feeling overcome by negative thoughts and feelings, you may begin to fear you are going insane. This is an extremely frightening experience. You might consider killing yourself as a way to escape the terrible sensations. Psychological pain can be much worse than physical pain.

When I was ten years old, I experienced many changes in my life all at once. My parents got divorced, my second brother went away to college, my father had a stroke, and we moved. My mother was very confused, and I felt alone in the world. It was as if everything I depended on had disappeared, and there was nothing to hold on to. I felt no one was there to help me understand my feelings, so I pushed them deep inside of myself. At night I had anxiety attacks. I would shake all over and feel as if I was being pulled into a pit. It was horrifying, especially because I had no idea what caused these feelings or what they were about. This experience went on for many months, and for years I wondered what had been happening to me.

Dr. Joan Borysenko, a best-selling author and therapist, refers to this type of experience as a "dark night of the soul". In her book, *Fire in the Soul*, she writes, "Dark nights of the soul are extended periods of dwelling at the threshold when it seems as if we can no longer trust the very ground we stand on, when there is nothing familiar left to hold onto that can give us comfort. If we have a strong belief that our suffering is in the service of growth, dark night experiences can lead us to depths of psychological and spiritual healing and revelation…"[1]

Looking back, I can see that my experience taught me many things. For one thing, it set me on a lifetime course of looking for spiritual answers to many deeply felt questions. Later in life when I experienced other difficult times, the essential knowledge I gained became a sort of rock that I could always rely on.

---

[1] Page 62. Joan Borysenko, *Fire in the Soul*. New York: Warner Books, 1993.

If you are having suicidal feelings, you are experiencing your own "dark night of the soul". This means you are becoming more open to philosophical answers. Hopefully, this chapter will begin to address some of your inner questions.

Remember Suicide Does Not End Suffering

When I read something that is common to many religions and beliefs of wise people, I feel convinced that it is true. *The Tibetan Book of the Living and Dying* by Soygul Rinpoche is a great source of information on what happens after you die, and it deals with many basic truths that are common to several religions. It is based on the knowledge of Tibetan monks and is fascinating reading.

According to Soygul Rinpoche, when you take your own life, you don't escape suffering. You are still alive on another plane of reality. You are not in your physical body in the same way, of course, but you have your same level of understanding and your same feelings. Unfortunately, your suffering goes with you. You still need to discover the truth, the way out, the source of true happiness and peace of mind. Suffering on earth and suffering on other planes all have the same goal—to help you find that inner core, deep inside of you. It is a place where you feel safe and happy no matter what happens externally.

The movie, *What Dreams May Come,* paints a colorful picture of what happens after you die. Have you seen it? The leading female character becomes so downhearted that she commits suicide. As the story illustrates, she does not escape her suffering by doing this, but only ends up in a worse condition. It is very painful to watch her go through so much turmoil. I wished she could have learned her lessons on earth in an easier way.

Every Experience Has a Lesson for You

Finding the inner Self is not just fancy philosophical talk, it is a natural process that all life and all experience are leading you towards, if you let it. It is as if the universe and true happiness are calling you home in every good and bad thing that happens to you. Nothing happens arbitrarily. There is a lesson for you in all your experiences. Your job is to figure out what the lessons are and so to become stronger and stronger. I believe that the universe wants you to be truly happy. When you experience suffering, it is not as a punishment, but to get your attention, to teach you something new, so you will finally move forward. Sometimes you can become very stuck and stop progressing. You take drugs, drink alcohol, or look for love from unloving sex. Then instead of getting better, you get worse. The suffering increases. This means the universe is starting to yell at you. "Wake up! Start learning the truth. Come back to the happiness you felt so naturally as child." If there wasn't emotional suffering, people wouldn't learn. It is the universe's way of helping you, although it often doesn't feel like it.

How You Can Make Yourself Feel Better Instantly

If you find yourself in a state of deep depression, there are several ways to help yourself. The most important thing to remember first is that inside of you, in a place you are temporarily out of touch with, is your inner Self. Spiritual teachers, like Jesus or Buddha have "realized the Self" and are continually in a state of complete peace and happiness called bliss. When you are seriously depressed, I think it helps to remind yourself that this place exists inside of you. There is no one on earth, even the most desperate criminal, who is not shining with love and light deep on the inside. You are, *in essence*, a truly perfect being. The following (written by a meditation teacher) is a wonderful description of the inner Self. Practice reading it whenever you feel down and want to remember who you really are. When you begin to really understand it, it will bring you a lot of comfort and a feeling of safety.

"The Self is that in us which knows all that is known and sees all that is seen. It is eternal, having no beginning or end…Since it is eternal, it is changeless. It was exactly the same before we inhabited this body, it was the same within us as an infant, as a young child, as a teenager, as a young adult, and no matter how old we get…it eternally remains the same. It does not get sick, grow old, or die. It is the *only* thing in this world that *never* changes. Everything else constantly changes all the time. This is who we are. This is our own true Self. We were never anything else."[2]

It would be great if you could push a button and suddenly feel that wonderful sense of safety inside yourself, but unfortunately, it does take some work to get there. The first thing you can do physically to feel better right away is to clear your mind a little. One of the biggest sources of feeling depressed is very dark, negative thoughts. You feel they are true, but I can promise you, they are not. In order to clear your mind, do the following:

1. Take ten long deep breaths. *When you breathe in, feel your abdomen expand.* This actually increases the life force inside of you. When you breathe out, imagine all your painful feelings leaving you. Imagine you feel warmer and happier. Imagine a wise person who loves you very deeply is sitting near you. Or imagine your favorite pet is sitting on your lap or at your feet. Imagination is a very powerful force. Einstein once said, "Imagination is more powerful than knowledge." When you use imagination positively, it can really make you feel better. Try this now. You can do it anytime during the day to help you feel more comfortable.

---

[2] Page 2. Volume 6, lesson 33. Ram Butler, *In Search of the Self.* South Fallsburg, New York: Syda Foundation, 1996.

2. Now watch your thoughts. Whenever a negative thought arises, look at it as if from a distance. Then replace it with a positive thought. For example, "I am so fat and ugly" could be replaced with "I am a beautiful girl. I have so many wonderful qualities." Even if you don't believe the positive thought at the time, and you think, "This is ridiculous. I'm lying to myself", do it anyway. This practice will lift your mood up. This is known as using positive affirmations. The truth is that there are two sides to every coin. Even though at the moment you feel one side is truer than the other, that is not the reality. Is one side of a dime truer than the other side?

3. Often when a young woman is very depressed, she will isolate herself. A better solution would be to find someone to talk to. This could be a friend, a counselor or even a hotline. Tell them about the advice you just read. Tell them your heavy thoughts and ask their help in replacing them with more life-loving thoughts. They can do the same thing with some of their own thoughts. Sharing and connecting with another person will improve your mood, because it shows you that you are a part of the universe and the family of humankind. When you stop feeling so alone, you feel better. It is human nature, and I believe, especially feminine nature, to want to connect to others.

Alcohol will Make You Feel Worse

If you notice you get very depressed when you drink, stay away from drinking. Drink virgin drinks instead or sip one drink slowly over a long period. Alcohol is a depressant, so if you lean towards depression anyway, don't help yourself farther down the road of sadness and negativity. The more you drink, the more difficult it is to bring yourself up out of a down mood in the ways I have just described.

Most people drink because they like to feel less inhibited than when they were sober. You can learn to be less inhibited with practice without drinking. Notice yourself when you drink. How is your personality different? Can you imagine yourself being that way without drinking? Try. Imagine yourself saying what you really want to say. Imagine yourself feeling relaxed and confident. You can do all of these things without drinking, just through practice and imagination.

If you notice you are much angrier when you drink than when you are sober, you need to think about that. What are you really angry about? Angry feelings may be your body's way of telling you there is some action you need to take, or you may need to root out some feelings and make an attitude adjustment of some sort. If you are angry about the way you were treated by someone in the past, you need to discover what the bad experience had to teach you and then you need to drop the past. (There is more about this later in the book.) If you don't look the sources of your anger squarely in the face, they will keep cropping up again and again. It is no fun to live the same anger and bad experiences over and over again, but many of us do, since it takes some courage to resolve these issues directly.

I knew a woman who was sexually abused as a child. The memory of her bad experiences kept reviving in her dreams and in her unhealthy relationships with others. She spent a lifetime running from her inner turmoil. Once I happened to suggest she read a particular book about people with similar experiences. She said she couldn't do it because it made her feel sick. She preferred to look the other way and keep stuffing her feelings back inside. Her life seemed to keep going in circles, until when she finally died, she was still in the same confused and tormented mental state. Perhaps if she had been able to find the courage to examine her past and the feelings that came from it, with the help of a therapist or friend, she could have finally healed and become freer and happier.

Healing Deeper Down

This chapter is designed to help you deal with depressed feelings in an emergency sort of way. In the next chapter I will be talking about how to help yourself in a deeper, more permanent way. If you find yourself feeling suicidal from time to time, as I have said, the universe is trying to tell you something. It is your work to find out what it is. Swami Muktananda, an Indian meditation master, offers the following advice, "You are not what you appear to be on the outside. You are something else on the inside, so discover that. Within a person there is the effulgence of God; each of you should see that radiance. Along with this light of God, there is so much joy. The purpose of human life is to attain that joy."[3] Realizing the Self is the essential purpose for all people, not just those who are suicidal. Young women with suicidal tendencies are people who now have a more urgent need to know their own Selves. In a way, these painful feelings are really a great blessing. Jesus once said, "Blessed are those that are poor in spirit, for theirs is the kingdom of heaven." I think the expression, "poor in spirit" means feeling empty and lost. Those in this state of mind are more motivated than most to seek out wisdom, because of their pain. It may be one of the reasons you are reading this book, for example.

So, how do you go about working on yourself, in order to become lighter and happier, the way you felt on a wonderful day as a child? This is a lifetime process, and it is one you can start right away. There are many methods to help you free yourself, and I would like to tell you about some of them in the next chapter.

---

[3] Page 107. Swami Chidvilasanda, *My Lord Loves a Pure Heart*. New York: UBS Publishers, 1994.

Three

How Can I Find My True Self?

You may have gotten the impression from parents or teachers that the main point to your life is to get good grades so that you can get a job. While this is an important goal in the young adult years, I feel it is not your most fundamental reason for living. In fact, acquiring lots of education can have the effect of building up your ego and take you even farther away from compassion for others and peace of mind. I am not saying that academic learning is not important, it is a very valuable discipline. If you want a stimulating job working with creative, educated people, getting a college education is a necessary first step in our society. However, I want you to realize that though a college degree can be an important life goal, from a broader perspective, it should not be your first priority. As Ralph Waldo Emerson once wrote back in 1831, "The things taught in colleges and schools are not an education, but the *means* of education."

When I was in college, I had no understanding of this basic truth. I was successful at studying, but grew more distant from my inner Self and more unhappy. I had no idea what I was doing all this work for, and my life seemed fairly pointless. Around the age of twenty-two, I began to read books about the Self by the psychologist, C.G. Jung. I also discovered *Autobiography of a Yogi,* the first book I ever read by a meditation master. I especially loved this book because it opened up a whole new world of thought for me.

I began to get a glimpse of the fact that the purpose of life is to grow more enlightened, stronger, happier, and more full of love. I felt far from being truly happy, but at least I was beginning to understand that this was what life was for, and that there were ways to move in that direction. This information seemed to be somehow outside of the realm of what I was taught in school. In the following sections I would like to share with you what I have learned over the span of my life so far about growing towards a higher level.

Learning from Other People

Everyone who comes into your life has something to teach you about yourself. If you find that one of these people makes you get angry a lot, for example, this is great material for you to think about. Why does this person have the power to get under your skin? Does he or she remind you of someone you knew when you were younger?

At one time I was a preschool director, and I started noticing that I often hired people who were like my mother. I had had a rocky relationship with my mother, so consciously this was not the kind of relationship I really wanted to repeat. I found myself relating to these women in the same sort of way I related to my mother. Once I woke up to the pattern I was repeating I had the opportunity to change the way I was acting. I believe the universe puts uncomfortable relationships in our life repeatedly in this way, so that we have a chance, often again and again, to finally do it right and act more harmoniously. Once I saw what was happening, I could practice ways that were healthier. When I became more aware, I also stopped hiring women that had the same sort of problems my mother had.

Here's another example my daughter gave me. A boy she knows has a knack of finding her weaknesses, the things she is most critical of about herself, and pointing them out to her. She finally began to realize that this was life's way of showing her how hard she is on herself about her appearance. She practiced supporting herself more whenever he would pick on her. She also realized why he was doing this. In general, he felt bad about his own many weak areas and was trying to build himself up by putting her down. I think this kind of interaction is very common among teenagers.

Take a moment to think. Who in your life makes you feel angry repeatedly? Does the person give you the same feelings you had as a child around someone else? How can you change the situation? Think creatively. Maybe you are choosing a wrong person to be around, simply because it gives you a familiar feeling. Often women, who were abused by their fathers, choose similar men as boyfriends or husbands. It is not that they consciously want to be unhappy, it is that people simply seek what is familiar. Know that you don't have to repeat your childhood experiences over and over.

In order to change these old patterns, it is necessary to become aware of them. Then you can learn from them and eventually drop them. *It is possible to rise above these negative experiences and start new.* First you need to look these feelings and experiences fully in the face. Once you are aware of where a negative pattern comes from, and you have felt the feelings that go along with it, you are then ready to drop it. As the meditation master, Swami Muktananda has said, "Drop the past!" It is simple advice, yet very profound. Look for more on how to drop the past later in the book.

Self-Respect

Ideally, all women should respect and love themselves. This is great ideal, but unfortunately, many women do not know *how* to respect themselves very much. I think this comes from our long history of being thought of as second class citizens or even as mere property. For centuries, we have been viewed as unstable, emotional creatures that needed the wisdom of men in the form of fathers, husbands, church elders, etc…for guidance. Naomi Weisstein, an American psychologist, writes, "How are women characterized in our culture and in psychology? They are inconsistent, emotionally unstable, lacking in strong conscience or super ego, weaker, "nurturant" rather than productive, "intuitive" rather than intelligent, and if they are at all "normal," suited to the home and the family. In short, the list adds up to a typical minority group stereotype of inferiority."[1] Is it any wonder that most women have low self-esteem?

In relation to our long history of being on this earth, it is new concept for us to learn how to stand on our own two feet, find our own voices, and show ourselves respect. This is especially difficult if we come from a family whose beliefs about women are still rooted in the past. You may have grown up with a father who still treats you like a little girl. Or your mother may value your physical appearance and your ability to attract a man over most of your other qualities. Breaking away from these family influences can be very challenging, but it can be done!

I believe young women need to spend time learning how to value their bodies, minds and feelings in a new way. (The new few chapters will go into this subject in more detail.) Again I would like to emphasize that you may not have been taught how to do this by your parents, your school or your culture (such as through television or movies). Since the atmosphere around you has not supported you in the direction of true self-respect, it is only natural that you may have become confused. I feel this is one reason such an overwhelming number of young women are depressed or have eating disorders. So the first thing to realize is that if you are unhappy now, you have a lot of company, and it is a natural result of the "climate" you live in presently.

Self-Reflection

There are many ways to practice self-reflection. One of my favorites is to write in a journal. Just write whatever comes to mind. It's not necessary to write in a polished or even grammatical way if you don't feel like it. The point is to allow thoughts and feelings room to surface. I often find that a more positive inner voice comes through when I write than does when I

---

[1] Page 544. Naomi Weisstein, "Psychology Constructs the Female". *The Norton Reader*. New York: W.W. Norton and Co., 1984.

am simply thinking. I also feel I can look at my feelings more as a detached observer when I see them on paper. My daughter says when she writes her feelings down, she sort of unloads her brain, so she can finally stop thinking about something. Afterwards, she feels freer to move on. Writing a journal is one of my most comforting personal habits. I always feel more settled afterwards.

If you don't think you'd like to write, you might try talking to a tape recorder and listening to it yourself or sending it to a friend. Again, this has the result of helping you see your thoughts and feelings from a distance and so helps you feel more in control.

Another form of self-reflection is simple contemplation. Just sit quietly by yourself and think about your friends, your family, your feelings and your goals. Really watch your thoughts from a centered place inside of yourself. Are they negative or positive? Do they lift you up or bring you down? Replace the negative with the positive, in the same way you would pull a weed out of a garden and plant a flower instead. Thinking the same old negative thoughts over and over until you feel worse is not contemplation. That will not move you to a higher level of happiness and truth.

Meditation

Learning how to meditate is an essential tool in your search for true feelings of happiness. Even if you get whatever you think you want, maybe a new car or the boyfriend you have always sought, you will not be happy if your mind torments you.

Mediation is as natural as breathing. You shouldn't think of it as something too mysterious or mystical that only monks in India do. It is simply a way of calming your thoughts so that you can watch them and begin to feel more peaceful.

To begin, sit cross-legged on the floor. Keep your spine straight but at ease. Begin to watch your breathing. Don't do anything to change your breathing. Just watch it. You will also notice lots of your thoughts coming and going. Don't try to not think. Imagine your thoughts are like clouds in a blue sky. The wind moves them gently along. The thoughts come in, and they go out. Just let them do that. When you breathe in, mentally say the word, "Ham", (with a soft \a\ sound) and when you exhale, say "so". This is a mantra that has been used by people for many centuries to quiet the mind. I believe it is filled with a powerful energy to help and protect you. By repeating it in this way with your breath, your mind will have something to hold on to. (If you prefer, You can use other phrases or words as a mantra, such as "peace" or "God loves me" or "I am the Self".) Eventually after a lot of practice, most of your thoughts will disappear, and you will only hear the mantra. The natural joy that exists in all of us will begin to fill you, and you will be on the road to a lasting sense of inner simplicity.

Begin by practicing meditation once a day for 10 to 20 minutes. After you really begin to enjoy the feeling it gives you, move to two times a day for 20 minutes each time. You can also meditate by lying flat on your back in bed. Try meditating in this way when you wake up or are falling asleep. Meditating right before you fall asleep will help you to sleep more restfully.

Learning how to meditate really deeply is a lot like learning how to play a musical instrument. You need to practice every day. You can't just pick up a violin and begin to play beautifully. Your mind is another kind of instrument. If you practice meditation nearly every day for twenty to thirty minutes, you will become better and better at watching your mind. You will notice your thoughts drifting away from the mantra all the time. Simply keep bringing them back to the mantra. Don't be hard on yourself. Everyone's mind does this. As you practice, your mind will have less thoughts when you meditate. No one can eliminate all her thoughts right away.

After you get the habit of practicing meditation regularly, you will find something wonderful will happen. You will be walking around doing your normal daily activities, and your mind will spontaneously become more still. *Whenever the mind is fairly still, you feel great. Feelings of love or joy sort of bubble up from inside you.* When this happens very consistently, you have reached a high level of awareness known as bliss.

If you are interested in more detailed information on how to meditate, do yoga stretches or breathing exercises, read Dr. Joan Borysenko's book, *Minding the Body, Mending the Mind.* She gives the reader clear and simple instructions in all these areas. Also, a meditation organization called Siddha Yoga offers courses that will help you learn these practices. Please see the resource section at the end of this book.

Change the Focus from Me to Others

If you are feeling down about yourself or your life in general, there is one surefire solution. Find a way to help other people. There is an expression, "God is busy helping you while you are busy helping others." I have really found that to be true. I was very self-involved when I graduated college. I had spent most of my time studying and thinking, hanging out with friends and thinking about me. My first job was teaching high school equivalency. As I began to help and turn my thoughts to what others were experiencing, I felt more connected to the human race somehow. My life problems seemed much smaller in relation to this new perspective. I felt stronger and more needed.

The wonderful thing is every city and high school or college campus has organizations that can help you find volunteer positions. Churches and other spiritual organizations are also sources of great opportunities. Often these helping occupations lead to salary-paying jobs as well. The job I just mentioned was the result of volunteering first as a tutor for underprivileged students. So even if you are unable to find a job right away that helps people, you can at begin the process by volunteering, at least for a few hours a week.

If you are depressed, really consider this suggestion. When you begin to help other people, God helps you by showing you strengths inside yourself you may not have known you possessed. You may discover you are a patient person or a good listener. Your newfound positive way of thinking may lift someone's mood. You may find you have a knack for organizing or telling funny stories. Your self-esteem grows when you notice others are benefited by your influence. As you share yourself, others share themselves and a sense of belonging arises.

Using work as a part of the process of Self-realization is known in Hindu philosophy as Karma Yoga. Part of that philosophy is the idea that bad karma you may have produced for yourself in the past is partly erased by performing good actions. The Methodist religion also places a strong emphasis on the benefits of doing "good works". As my husband once taught me, the great part about helping others is that you end up helping yourself at the same time. However, he pointed out, if you just help yourself, no one else benefits.

In one episode of the TV series, *Friends,* Joey tries to convince Phoebe that there are really no purely selfless good deeds. In other words, whenever you help others, you always end up benefiting yourself as well. She tries and tries to do a completely selfless action to prove him wrong, but always finds she gets something back in return. I know you will notice the same effect!

Practicing Mindfulness

This practice is a lot like meditation, but you do it when you're simply living your daily life. It refers to learning how to live fully in the present moment. Have you ever noticed how happy you feel when you go on vacation? One of the reasons you feel that lightness is that your thoughts have decreased. You are not thinking about what you are supposed to do that day. You are not planning and attempting to control your schedule.

Your mind is simply free and clear. You are living more in the moment. It is really not the vacation that makes you happy. It is the clear, at ease mind.

A Western journalist once asked Gandhi, "Mr. Gandhi, you have been working at least fifteen hours a day, every day, for almost fifty years. Don't you think it's about time you took a vacation?"

"Why?" Gandhi said, "I am always on vacation."[2]

The way to feel like you are always on vacation is to learn the art of mindfulness. Mindfulness means that when you are doing something, for example, washing dishes, you only do that one thing. You give it your full and total attention. Your mind becomes quieter. You feel your whole body. You really see the dish. You feel the temperature of the water. You perform the task carefully. In this way, even the most everyday task becomes a meditation. Again, like meditation, this takes practice.

I once watched a monk lift a glass and take a drink of water. I could tell he was practicing mindfulness. He appeared very cheerful and focused. He lifted the glass slowly. He swallowed carefully. He seemed present to the moment and very happy.

Try mindfulness today. Choose one of your simple daily tasks. You will be so amazed at how good it feels to focus on one thing and one thing only. You may even notice that your breathing naturally becomes deeper and slower. When you are fully in the moment, your whole body will become more at ease. There is a Zen (eastern philosophy) saying, "When you eat, eat. When you drink, drink." In the beginning you may remember to do this only once or twice a day. After you begin to really enjoy it, you will do it more often. The trick is to remember to do it. Don't forget! Try it today.

---

[2] Eknath Easwaran, *Ghandi the Man*. California: Nilgiri Press, 1983.

Jessica adds that she likes to practice mindfulness when she is eating a piece of chocolate cake. In this way she really enjoys that cake and the experience seems to last longer.

Also, practice being mindful when you are with another person. Really notice that person. Listen carefully to what they are saying. Completely be with them. The person will really appreciate it. We all enjoy lots of attention. You may notice this single-minded focus brings you a sense of love and lightness, and that a feeling of love will often be returned to you. This is the result of being in the moment and at ease with yourself.

The opposite of mindfulness is the habit of doing many things at once. You have probably experienced what it feels like to talk on the phone, eat a sandwich, and get dressed all at the same time. In our fast-paced modern climate, this kind of "efficiency" is commonplace. And have you ever experienced talking to someone, when their mind is on a hundred other subjects? There is no sense of joy in that kind of conversation.

Mindfulness also has some amazing physical benefits. Ellen Langer, a Harvard psychologist, found in her experimental studies that enhanced mindfulness can "improve people's health, reverse memory loss, increase brain development, improve eyesight and hearing, reduce depression, increase self-confidence, and lengthen a person's life".[3] Doesn't that sound wonderful?

If you would like to read more about the concept of mindfulness, there are some book suggestions in the resource section at the back of this book.

Watching Your Words

The way you use your words has a huge effect on how you feel and how others feel around you. The best advice I ever heard about how to speak comes from an eastern religion known as Sufiism. It goes something like,

---

[3] Page 13. Letty Cottin Pogrebin, *Getting Over Getting Older*. New York: Berkley Books, 1996.

"Be sure that your words pass through each of these three gates: Is it necessary? Is it truthful? Is it kind?"

The first part of the Sufis' advice ("Is it necessary?") means you should reflect before you speak on whether or not this is something that really needs to be said. Are you just talking to make noise and hear your own voice? Are you elaborating on a point that you really already made? If you choose your words carefully, instead of pouring them out whenever you speak, you will accomplish many things. For one, you will save yourself a lot of energy. Talking all day in a useless way can really drain you. It will also sap the energy of the people around you. If you use fewer words, you also have a better chance of meeting your next two goals of speaking honestly and kindly. It is very difficult to watch what you say, if a flood of words pours out every time you speak.

If you attempt to always say what is true, you are practicing being truer to yourself and more authentic with others. I remember an old *I Love Lucy* show in which her friends bet her she could not tell the truth for so many hours. It was very difficult for her at first, because, like many women, she was so used to pleasing others and telling people what they wanted to hear. After doing it for awhile, she really began to enjoy a whole new sense of freedom. In the movie, *Sex, Lies and Videotape*, one of the leading characters had decided to always speak the truth. Whenever he said something, it was such a refreshing contrast to the way another leading male character always lied. For me, his vow of total honesty was the main reason the movie seemed fascinating.

If you are a typical female people-pleaser, don't expect that you can change this habit right away. I am still working on it myself. I grew up thinking my job was to listen to everyone's problems. I was especially good at being quiet so I wouldn't get it anyone's way. It took many years for me to learn how to express my thoughts and feelings no matter what anyone else's opinion about them was.

While speaking truthfully is an important part of being a "real person", I am not advocating that you be brutally truthful all the time. As the Sufis advise, also be kind. There are many ways to say what you need to say. Get your point across, but in a loving way, if possible. If you have the perfect balance between respecting yourself and respecting others in what you say, you have really accomplished something!

I have taught Suzuki piano lessons for many years. That method taught me the following practice. When I need to make a suggestion to a parent or a student about changing some behavior, I first give the student some praise on something he did right. In this way the student feels good about himself and receives the advice more easily. I never offer fake praise. I talk about something that I genuinely want to encourage. Being honest and kind at the same time is a skill, and, like many of the practices we have been discussing, it requires practice. Don't expect to be able to do it completely right away, but you can feel good knowing you are heading in a positive direction.

Unfortunately, there are not many models for the art of watching your words in the mass media. Television and movies are packed with examples of people using their words to express dishonesty and meanness. However, if you really look for them, there are some examples of compassionate, honest and careful speakers. One example I can think of is the two characters played by Tim Robbins and Morgan Freeman in *Shawshank Redemption*. Their caring friendship is consistently revealed in their simple and direct conversations. Maybe you can think of some other good examples in movies you have seen recently.

Learn the Art of "A Little Every Day"

Think of something you would like to accomplish. Maybe you would like to be a dancer in a dance company or be able to play the guitar. Perhaps it is your dream to become a lawyer or a writer. Here's how. Start by doing a little every day in the direction of your goal. If it is your dream to be a dancer, today just look up some dance schools in your area. If money is an issue, begin by saving something towards that end. If you think you are too fat, begin by starting an exercise program. Beginning is usually the most difficult step. Once you have done that, resolve that you will do a small action every day to move in that direction. You will be surprised how much better you feel about your life in general just to know you are moving towards one of your dreams. It is an exciting and encouraging feeling.

Right now one of my dreams is to be able to play classical guitar really beautifully so that I can perform for others, maybe in restaurants. Every day I practice for just a half hour, and I listen to guitar tapes in my car. I'm not spending a lot of time on it because I am also working and doing other things. However, I really enjoy watching my progress, and I like to fantasize about the wonderful music I will be able to play.

It doesn't matter how fast you are progressing. It may take me several years before I can play some of the pieces I would like to be able to play. Remember the story of the tortoise and the hare? The slow turtle ended up beating the rabbit in the race, simply because his progress was steady. The moral of the story was "Slow and steady wins the race." Just keep moving forward, and always keep your goal in mind. You will be amazed at how much closer you are to a goal if you really commit yourself to doing a little each day.

The Company You Keep

There are so many powerful influences on your thoughts and feelings. One of the most powerful is the people you come in contact with. They have the ability to bring you up or take you down. These influences include your family, your friends and the mass media.

If you come from a healthy, loving family, you are a very fortunate person. The ideal parents offer advice, yet allow their young adult children room to make their own decisions. They are always available to listen to you when you have problems. They encourage you to pursue your dreams. They know how to love you and to let go of you at the same time. They are also role models of ethical, creative and happy adults.

If this sounds nothing like your parents, don't worry. You are not alone. Many young adults do not have ideal parents. You are at the point in your life where you begin to see that your parents are just human beings and need to work on themselves just as much as you do. *If you find your parents make you feel worse about yourself and seem to pull you in a negative direction, find other adults to be your role models.* They could be teachers, spiritual leaders, or parents of friends. If you really feel the need for older mentors, they are all around you if you look for them.

One of the most important influences on your thoughts and feelings in the early adult years is your friends. Choose them carefully. If you notice your friends help you with the positive changes you are trying to make in your life, keep them. If your friends seem to keep tempting you to go in the opposite direction, even though it may be very difficult, you should look for new friends. If you live away from your family now, your friends become your new family. They should watch out for you and help you grow. You can do the same for them. Hopefully, your friends can provide you with a wonderful example of how to live. They may not be perfect, but like you, they should be working to respect their bodies, minds and souls in every possible way.

Another type of company that you keep is what you read and watch. Everything affects you in some way, especially in your time of life when you are working so hard to discover who you really are. If you frequently watch talk shows on TV, you will be filled with thoughts from very confused people. If you often watch horror movies, you will absorb the minds of psychotics. If you watch TV shows about soap opera melodramas, you will tend to view life as an emotional roller coaster. Choose this type of company carefully. Find books, movies and shows that help you move forward, that inspire you and make you laugh. There is so much that you can learn from the mass media, but you need to watch if it is causing you to become more positive or more destructive.

Know That Discipline Brings Freedom

This is a thought you really need to understand. It is not a very popular idea right now I think. Most people think that discipline is a dry and up-tight sort of word. It somehow makes you think of the military or of feeling very stiff. However, everyone wants to feel free. We all agree that sounds like a lot of fun.

Think how wonderful it would be to have the freedom of a gymnast or runner in the Olympics, winning a gold medal. How great to be a jazz musician, jamming with friends. How stimulating it would be to have a creative job working with fascinating and brilliant co-workers. These activities all represent a certain freedom and joy, but they are also not possible without discipline. In order to be an athlete in the Olympics, for example, you would need to train every day. Also, in order to find yourself in a creative and inspiring work environment, you would first need to develop skills.

Please drop false hopes of being suddenly discovered and handed a job as a fashion model or actress, for example. This rarely happens, and when it does, it can disappear quickly. However, do have dreams and fantasies, but make them ones you can really work towards. And remember you can accomplish almost anything if you decide to take one step at a time and work just a little every day. It takes a little self-discipline and courage, and I know you have that if you understand its value.

A few years ago I decided I wanted to start writing books. I liked to imagine seeing them published and reading people's letters about them. Getting motivated to actually write was the challenging part. To tell you the truth, I never really felt like it. This is where I had to gather some self-discipline, the willingness to do something even though I didn't feel like doing it. I decided to just write about a page a day. Just a page didn't seem like too much work, and I figured that after about three months, I'd have a short book. The whole process of getting the book published, etc…took much longer, but the challenging part was accomplished fairly easily. Now I have developed a habit, which makes the writing of future books even more effortless. Nearly every morning I do a little writing. The rest of the day I have a good feeling—that I made some progress that day towards manifesting one of my dreams.

Dharma

Dharma is a word that comes from Sanskrit, a language from India. One amazing thing about Sanskrit is that it offers us hundreds of words and expressions that describe concepts about our inner life and self-realization. Dharma roughly translated means "duty". It means a lot more than just that, which is why I am bothering to use a word from another language.

If you follow your dharma, it means you try to listen to what your deepest inner voice wants you to do and then do it. All great beings practice dharma. When Jesus said, "Thy will, not mine, be done," he was talking about his desire to work for God, not for his own ego. Having known in advance that he would be persecuted, he could have run away from the situation. It was his desire to follow God's will that kept him from leaving. Joan of Arc is another example of someone who listened to her inner voice in order to discover the best actions to take. She said she would rather have stayed at home, sewing with her mother. Instead, due to her belief in following her inner directions, she led an army courageously into many bloody battles. As you can see, following your dharma involves developing the ability to listen to your inner voice and also the courage to do what it tells you.

The first step is to listen to your inner voice. If your mind is chattering on and on, like the commercials on TV, you will not be able to distinguish your wise inner voice from that of some other influence. This is where meditation comes in. Practice meditation every day. When your mind begins to quiet, even just a little, you will often receive answers to your questions and suggestions on what course of action to take next.

In any given moment, if you are considering which of two actions to take, say, go to a friend's house or go to a party, ask yourself which would bring you closer to knowing your true self. Or ask yourself if a wise person were with you right now, what would he or she suggest you do. When you follow the highest choice of action at any moment, you are following a dharmic path.

What is a dharmic choice for one person may not necessarily be a dharmic choice for someone else. There are no black and white answers in this area. In one person's case, divorce or abortion, for example, could be the right choice of action. For another person, the decision to have a divorce or an abortion could be totally wrong and bring many negative consequences. As you practice listening to your inner wisdom, what is right for you becomes more and more obvious.

This is another concept that requires practice. Don't be discouraged if you feel you can't do it right away. You may have a good understanding of what is the right thing to do in a situation. For example, you know you should pass on that greasy, pepperoni pizza, since you resolved to eat more healthy foods last week. However, at the time, you lack the courage or will power. Will power is just like a muscle. You have to keep using it to build it up. Keep coming back to it. In time you will develop more ability.

Or you may have more trouble just knowing what the best course of action at the time is for you. Start to observe the results of your decisions. Actions that in the long run make you feel stronger and more content are most likely dharmic actions. Actions that weaken and discourage you are not. Eating well and exercising daily is dharmic. Drinking lots of beer regularly and sleeping twelve hours a day is not.

The more you consciously practice doing dharmic actions, the more meaningful your life will become. The more I started listening to the directions of my inner Self, the more I felt my inner Self wanted to reach me too. I have often had the experience of finding just the book I needed at the time when I was browsing in the bookstore. Or a dream will come to me and answer some questions I was asking. Sometimes I have had a prayer answered by an unexpected source. There are hundreds of ways the universe has of communicating with you. You only need to begin to listen.

This chapter was a sort of overview of the process of getting to know your true Self, which I believe is your highest purpose in life. The next several chapters will offer advice on specific subjects that are of interest to young women, such as relationships with friends and parents, health, worry and others. If you can understand and begin practicing some of the concepts in this chapter, I know you will notice many positive changes in all these other areas of your life. For this reason, in the following chapters I will continue to review many of the same themes just presented.

Four

How Can I Find Happiness in Relationships?

In this chapter I will be discussing relationships with others, specifically—
the opposite sex, other young women friends and your parents. The following are some thoughts I have shared with my daughter from time to time.

Sexual Relationships with Boys

First of all, there are psychological differences between boys and girls.
The book, *Men are from Mars, Women are from Venus* describes these differences in great detail. In many cases, girls are looking for love, connection and acceptance from a boyfriend. Initially, girls are more likely than
boys to want a committed relationship. On the other hand, boys in their
teens and early twenties are often looking for a more casual relationship
and for sex. (Of course, this is a broad generalization and does not apply
to all girls and boys.)

I think it is helpful for girls to understand this difference as they begin
their adolescent years. This understanding can make them less vulnerable
to being preyed on by boys who are talented at flattering and seeming to
give the love and acceptance girls are looking for. Often, in these cases,
after the boy gets the sex he is after, he no longer wants the relationship.

If you are really looking for a relationship or deeper friendship with a
boy, you need to develop this *first*, before having sex. Boys, in general,
enjoy the chase. The longer the chase is, the more time you have to get to
know each other and develop a sense of connection. Although girls, of

39

course, have a strong desire for sex, as boys do, this really is not their top priority. Young women need to be the ones with the superior self-control. They need to set the tone of the friendship.

Unfortunately, it is very common today for girls to have sex with boys they barely know. It's almost like the first kiss was thirty years ago. Sex has lost its deeper significance. It's what everybody does in the high school or college scene. Sadly, girls are the ones who suffer most with this modern philosophy.

For one thing, they lose their self-respect. A boy who has slept with many girls is just considered cool, but a girl begins to feel she is a "hoochie-mama", to use a current phrase. Although modern philosophy pretends to see boys and girls as equal in the sexual world, biologically, they still are not. Girls have to worry about being pregnant. This is a fact young women can never get around no matter how modern they are. For this reason, the sexual relationship has to carry more significance for a girl than it does for a boy. It has the potential for disastrous consequences. When a girl tries to ignore these two facts, loss of self-respect and putting herself in constant danger, she may begin to suffer in various ways.

The answer to this dilemma lies in developing your own inner wisdom and in learning to treat yourself with the greatest self-respect. Give sexual relations their full meaning. Give yourself the fullest respect. When you do decide to have sex with a boy, be sure you have known him for a long time. Be certain that you both see each other as real human beings with good and bad qualities. Ideally, wait until you both feel a deep sense of love and commitment towards each other. Think of sex as a way of expressing an already deep sense of connection, instead of as a way of trying to get more connected.

Girls often fall into this particular trap. They mistakenly think that sex will make the boy like them more, so they jump right into a sexual relationship. Although the boy wants sex, he may not necessarily want a relationship. When he sees that the girl feels more connected to him after sex, he may feel frightened he will be smothered and then run farther away. In this way, the relationships between boys and girls become more confused and unhappy.

If you have already been through some of the experiences just mentioned, don't be hard on yourself about it. It is very natural to be influenced by peers and the social climate that surrounds you. The best course of action now is to start over and simply drop the past. Begin fresh today. Start a new life with renewed self-respect this very moment. You are young and the rest of your life awaits you.

The Dalai Lama, a monk from Tibet who is respected around the world for his wise teachings, has said the following about sexual relationships:

"So it seems, then, that there can be two principal types of relationships based on sexual attraction. One type is based on pure sexual desire. In this case the motive or the impetus behind the bond really is just temporary satisfaction, immediate gratification. In that type of relationship, individuals are relating to each other not so much as people but rather as objects. That type of relationship is not very sound. If the relationship is based only on sexual desire, without a component of mutual respect, then the relationship becomes almost like prostitution, in which neither side has respect for the other. A relationship built primarily on sexual desire is like a house built on a foundation of ice; as soon as the ice melts, the building collapses.

"However, there is a second type of relationship which is also based on sexual attraction, but in which the physical attraction is not the predominant basis of the relationship. In this second type of relationship there is an underlying appreciation of the value of the other person based on your feeling that the other person is kind, nice, and gentle, and you accord respect and dignity to that other individual. Any relationship that is based on that will be much more long lasting and reliable. It's more appropriate. And in order to establish that type of relationship, it is crucial to spend enough time to get to know each other in a genuine sense, to know each other's basic characteristics.

"Therefore, when my friends ask me about their marriage, I usually ask how long they've known each other. If they say a few months, then I usually say, 'Oh, this is too short.' If they say a few years, then it seems to be better. Now they not only know each other's face or appearance but, I think, the deeper nature of the other person…"[1]

Love at First Sight?

Clearly there is infatuation at first sight, but I don't believe in love at first sight. It is very common for two people to feel strongly attracted to each other almost instantly. However, true love, the kind that lasts for many years, takes time to grow. This type of love is built on shared experiences, a sense of commitment and a willingness to learn and grow together.

I have known several couples who knew each other first as friends. There was no electric or passionate connection right in the beginning. Slowly, over time, as they grew to know each other, love eventually developed. This was my experience with my first love and with the man I eventually married.

I am not saying that a strong initial attraction will never lead to deeper love. Over time that is possible. I just want you to know that real love takes time. If you meet someone whom you basically like and respect give the relationship a chance. You never know what will develop as you get to know each other. You may be surprised!

When you are looking for someone to love, look for deeper qualities than just physical appearance and an attractive personality. You may find a "diamond in the rough", and as love grows, the person's best qualities may

---

[1] Pages 101-102. His Holiness the Dalai Lama and Howard C. Cutler, *The Art of Happiness.* New York: Riverhead Books, 1998.

be revealed. People are often not what they seem. A flashy exterior can mask a cruel being, and a shy image may later reveal a charismatic and creative soul. Take your time and look deep!

Non-sexual Friendships with Boys

I think it is wonderfully healthy for girls to have friendships with boys who are like brothers to them. This is a great way to get to know how the opposite sex thinks and feels without being too emotionally involved. In this type of relationship, boys and girls can learn to feel equal and to treat each other honestly and with respect. Later this understanding will help them develop happy marriages.

Our popular culture seems to give girls the message that their life is unsuccessful without a serious, sexual relationship with a boy. If a young woman has finished high school without having this kind of relationship, she often feels like a failure. Dr. Gilda Carle, a relationship therapist, wrote, "During their teen years, young women go through relationships as quickly as they change their underwear. If they feel they lack success in getting someone to love them, they question their self-esteem. Many girls actually leave for college thinking they're social failures because they haven't yet found love. And when these girls graduate four years later, despite the fact that they are actively pursuing important careers, many still feel that their #1 priority is to find the proverbial prince."[2]

I would like to promote another message for young women. If you have made progress learning about yourself, have had several respectful and honest relationships with boys and girls, and have made progress towards a career, you should consider yourself a great success. Even if you have accomplished only one of these goals, you have moved forward positively. Let's cancel the old value that finding a man is our main goal in life.

[2] Pages 9-10. Dr. Gilda Carle, *Women's Ten Big Worries...and How to Beat 'em.* Boca Raton, Florida: American Media Mini Mags, Inc.,2000.

Although a long-term relationship can be a very meaningful part of life, there are also many other worthy pursuits.

A Long-term Relationship

If you have already passed through the casual relationship stage and now find yourself in a serious, long-term relationship, there are a couple of important things I would like you to know. One is that a serious relationship goes through stages, and the second is that there is a deeper purpose for your relationship, other than sex and companionship.

Usually the first stage a committed relationship travels through is the famous "honeymoon stage". This is a wonderful time, when you look at each other through rose-colored glasses, seeing each other's best qualities and feeling very attracted and in love. This can be a magical time of life, so enjoy it to its fullest!

It is a wise person who knows that this child-like euphoria doesn't last forever. I want you to understand that this ending is a natural part of the deep relationship process, and nothing is going wrong. Many marriages have ended when the honeymoon stage ends. The couple feels the romance died so they must have made a wrong decision, and should move on looking for the next romance. This is not true!

After the honeymoon stage, comes the, let's call it, the "back to earth" stage. Life begins to assume a more everyday type quality. You begin to fall into a usual work routine, and sex may seem a little more simply affectionate and less passionate. Your mate begins to seem more and more like a regular human being and less like an angel.

And then comes the "first challenge" stage. Slowly and surely, each person's negative personal qualities begin to surface. And you may start having your first fights. This, too, is a natural part of the relationship process and leads us to a discussion of the deeper purpose of a long-term relationship.

There is a great book written by a marriage counselor who has worked with hundreds of couples over the years. It's called *Getting the Love You Want* by Harville Hendrix. It is the most down-to-earth discussion I've ever read of the differences between what a man looks for in a marriage and what a woman looks for. The author believes, as I do, that the purpose of marriage is to learn more about your Self and so evolve to a higher level. Once this process really begins in a marriage or a committed relationship, you may experience a lot of pain, irritation and other unpleasant qualities. Again, resist the idea that something is going wrong. This is just the way the universe has to get you back on the track of coming closer to your true Self.

For example, it is very common for women to marry someone like their own father. Most women have some psychological issues with their own father that they were unable to resolve as children. Your marriage then becomes a place where you get a second chance to resolve those problems. When I married my husband, the thought never occurred to me that he was like my father. My husband had been a monk in India and knew a lot about religion and eastern philosophy. My father had been a successful businessman and stockbroker, as well as a workaholic. To me they seemed poles apart. However, a few years after our marriage, my husband actually turned into that image of my father! He became a prosperous businessman, worked long hours, and he now even spends hours a day on the stock market.

As this example illustrates, often deeper, unconscious forces guide our choice of a mate. You may even find you have turned into the image of your own mother and often the mother of your mate. Recognizing what is happening is the first step. Once something becomes conscious, you have the power to change it. In my case, I was able to sort of rewrite one of the negative aspects of my own childhood. Since my father was always out of the home as a child, I never knew him. When my daughter was young, I was able to change the tendency for a distant relationship between father and daughter. Although my husband wasn't as involved in her childhood as would be ideal, he spent time with her every day and gradually became a meaningful influence on her life.

Since marriage has a way of bringing all our negative personal traits out into the open, many couples can't take the heat and run away from the relationship. The divorce rate in our country, for example, has skyrocketed in the last fifty years. People often feel they can find something better in another relationship. The trouble with this theory is that the issues you have carried with you from your childhood follow you into your next relationship. Then the same drama happens over and over again. No one really wants to spend her life going round and round in circles in this way, but this is often the case with those who run from relationship to relationship.

When you do decide to get married, do as the Dalai Lama recommends. Take as long a time as possible to get to know your potential future husband. Be sure this is someone you want to spend your lifetime with. Then if you decide to get married, make a commitment. You are not only committing to stay with that person, you are also committing to learn and evolve from the stresses that a deep relationship brings. Remember the purpose of your life. You are here to really grow and move forward to a higher level. Working to maintain a solid marriage is one of the most powerful tools life gives you to rework your past and become a stronger person. Discuss this concept with your future husband. If you are both fully conscious of the decision to stay together really "for better or worse" as the marriage vow says, the struggles of your marriage will make more sense to both of you.

If your own parents are divorced, it doesn't mean you have to follow the same pattern. As I have said earlier, you have the ability to heal the past and move forward. I remember my older brother telling me when I was in college that maybe we would never have good marriages because our parents were divorced. (From reading a recent *Time* magazine article about children of divorced parents, I think many young people worry about this issue.) However, both of us ended up finding good people to marry, and we both have been happily married to our spouses for close to twenty-five years now. I am mentioning this here, because I want you to know that the unsuccessful marriages of the generation before you are not a legacy you are compelled to continue.

The Ideal Attitude towards Your Mate

Once you have passed through the three relationship stages just discussed, what's next? I think your ultimate behavior goal in a relationship is to treat each other with the greatest love and respect. Ideally, you see your husband as your own inner Self. Deep on the inside he is the same person you are. Once you learn to treat yourself with love and respect, it will be only natural for you to do the same to him. This is the basis of any mature, healthy relationship. It may take time for you to reach this goal, but it is very helpful to know that is where you are heading. In the famous Indian chant entitled the *Gurugita*, the god, Shiva tells his beloved, Parvati, "You are my very Self." I think this is the most romantic phrase ever spoken between lovers. I hope you find this type of love.

It is my deepest hope that your generation will set a new trend of healthy, committed marriages. Our society clearly needs healing in this area. If you believe in the ideas just discussed, talk about them with your friends. Give your future children the comfort of having courageous, wise and affectionate parents who realize the true purpose of marriage and of life. You and your husband can be those parents. It only requires a little wisdom and a strong sense of commitment. You have the capacity for both, no matter what the conditions of your childhood were.

Lost Love

At some point in your life you will probably experience at least one heartbreak. It seems to be a very natural part of the growing up process. The word heartbreak is actually very appropriate, for when you lose a loving relationship, you may actually experience pain in the energy center (called Chakra) of your body that is near your heart. Many people experience an uncomfortable ache in their stomach as well, and so it is common to not feel hungry. If you experienced a lot of love and a deep sense of connection when you were in the relationship, you may now experience the opposite, a sense of emptiness and a sense of separation from life. In short, you are noticing the polarities of life, the ups and downs that make the movie of reality so fascinating.

Of course, being in pain doesn't seem so fascinating at the time. You may wonder when this will end. I think heartbreak is sort of like a virus. It has to run its course, which it will, and then you will feel better again.

In the meantime, here are some encouraging thoughts. First, know that this kind of pain is shared by many. It is universal. People have suffered from losing love in their life since the beginning of time

It is also helpful to know that the pain that comes from losing a loving relationship is like a fire. In yogic philosophy, this kind of inner fire burns away some of your misunderstanding about life. Through suffering in this way you are learning and eventually becoming a more mature person. I believe there is a lesson waiting to be learned in nearly every from of psychological pain, if you are willing to look for it.

This is the essential reason that taking medication or drinking alcohol to numb yourself is not such a good idea. If you continually numb yourself, you can't learn. Then you begin to simply go in circles instead of moving forward. And when you run from pain, you end up suffering more in the long run. In contrast, when you learn from your life lessons, your happiness continually increases.

Friendships with Girls

Again, your friendships with other girls are another way for you to learn more about yourself and evolve to a higher level in your personal growth.

When you develop a close relationship with someone, for example, your college roommate, the opportunity arises for you to see yourself as if in a mirror. Pay close attention to habits your roommate has that really irritate you. You may find you have the same qualities. Also, your roommate may hold up a more obvious mirror for you when you argue with each other. When you hear direct criticism from someone who is angry, your first urge is to reject the information. Your best move would be to reflect on what she told you when things quiet down. Her criticism may have had some truth in it, especially if it hurt when you thought about her words later. Reflect on it. Do you want to change something about yourself? Is this mirror showing you something you would rather not see? If you have the strength to look at criticism in this positive way, you will begin to grow faster, and your relationships with others will be stronger and more open.

From the opposite angle, you may be critical of something your friend does that annoys you. Say, for example, you think she lets boys treat her badly. You tell her this because you are tired of seeing her get hurt in this way, and you want to help her maybe because you have had similar experiences. You feel you want to help her see herself more clearly and break a negative habit. I think this is a positive urge, to want to help and give advice to others. However, now comes the tricky part. Your friend hears your advice, but she's not ready to accept it. She may even get angry about it. This is where you have to draw your line. You can not live anyone's life for her. If she is not ready to listen and to change, it is up to the universe to do the rest. Life is always the best teacher, and you can be sure that it will continue with its teaching assignment. After you've said your peace, you need to let go and accept the person with all their weaknesses. In the long run, your companionship and affection will do more for her than any advice ever can.

There is, however, one exception to this. If the friend's negative habits are so powerful and destructive that they are pulling you down, you need to leave the friendship. Say, for example, your friend is a heavy drinker. Every night you are out with her, she gets into arguments with others and does other destructive activities. You end up cleaning up the pieces of whatever happened. In this way, the friend's bad habits are negatively affecting your life. If the friend is not willing to change at all, you need to separate yourself by staying away from these negative situations. Accepting others as they are is a great virtue unless you are hurting yourself in the process. Developing the ability to discriminate between when to advise, when to accept and when to let go is an essential skill you can develop at your age. I can almost guarantee you that situations will arise in your life that will help you acquire this ability. It is one of your life lessons at this time.

Your Relationship with Your Parents

When you were a child, you looked up to your parents as sources of guidance and protection in every possible way. A young child has to trust and admire her parents, or perhaps older siblings, because they are her only means for survival at the time. Your childhood experience is just given to you. You can't possibly have any say over how it is going to go. Your only choice is to accept it, good or bad.

When you grow up, you have the ability to sort of "rewrite" parts of your childhood that were not as happy or healthy as you would have liked. Also, at your age, you are learning how to be your own parent, the kind of parent maybe you wish you had. You are also growing the power to think for yourself, no matter how your parents object. Going against the will of your parents can be frightening, but it is sometimes a necessary part of Self-realization.

A recent movie, *The Kid,* with Bruce Willis illustrates perfectly the concept of rewriting the unhappy parts of one's childhood. His inner child is constantly following the leading character (Bruce Willis) and annoying him until he finally goes back with the child to some painful childhood experiences. He can't stop the child from having those experiences, but this time he is with the child as a wise support person. In this way, the adult learned from his childhood difficulties and was able to heal and move forward. Bruce Willis's character was now able to pursue a lifelong career dream and to form a loving relationship with a woman. It was a very inspiring and positive movie!

You can do the same healing experience inwardly. Lie down and imagine one of your most painful childhood experiences. Go through the experience and feel all of the feelings, however uncomfortable. Picture your child self clearly. Also vividly imagine that you at your present age are there too. Hug the child and talk to her as you wish you could have been talked to back then. In this way, you are actually soothing the child that you carry with you wherever you go. This is a very powerful exercise. Do it and you will notice positive changes in your present life.

One of my painful childhood experiences was when my mother told me (around age ten) that we were moving, and that she and my father were getting a divorce. I started crying, and she became angry and said, "What are you crying for?" I felt embarrassed by my emotion and immediately stopped. I felt totally unsupported and alone. I think a part of me decided at that point that I was on my own and shouldn't ask for help from others. It was a sort of turning point in my life when I felt I suddenly became a pseudo-adult. It seemed that now I had to put away all childish emotions of weakness or vulnerability.

When I go back to that experience in my mind, I again experience all the same feelings. However, this time I rewrite it by being with the child as my wiser adult self. I treat my inner child as I would have treated my daughter when she was little. I hold my child and tell her she can cry as much as she wants. I say it is natural to feel upset with all the changes going on in her life. I explain that anyone would feel afraid and sad about a family breaking up and about leaving her home and school. I tell my child she is never alone because God and I are always with her in her heart. I give the child every bit of nurturing I was missing. When I did this exercise, I felt warmer and more loved instantly. Give it a try.

Although we can never take away our hurtful past experiences, we can work with them in a way that will make us more open and compassionate with others. When we face and heal the experiences that hurt us, we are then able to help others who have suffered in similar ways. If we refuse to rewrite these situations, the childhood dramas will continue to haunt us, and our relationships with others may be more destructive than loving.

If you cannot seem to retrieve *any* childhood memories, or very few, it is possible you have post-traumatic stress syndrome (PTSS). This happens when someone has suffered some form of extreme trauma as a child, such as emotional, sexual, or physical abuse. As a way of protecting herself and surviving these horrible experiences, the individual may have blocked all the memories of that time of life. Unfortunately, the effects remain, and the person may experience anxiety, nightmares, self-hatred, trouble in relating to others, and other symptoms.

If you feel your childhood may contain secrets that are still haunting you today, the best solution is to seek the help of an excellent therapist that you really admire and feel comfortable with. Talk to several therapists before deciding which one would be the best for you. Several techniques are available today that can help in retrieving these lost memories, such as hypnotism, REM simulation and past life regression.

If you have had a fairly traumatic relationship with your own parents, a therapist can help support you and be a kind of interim parent. Even if you have had healthy parents, the older you get, the more you become your own parent and begin to think for yourself. This process can be challenging for you and for your parents as well.

Let's take a minute to look at the parent's perspective. During most of the time they have known you, you were a child. It is very natural for them to still look at you as a child. In fact, when you are a teenager, you fluctuated between acting in an adult way and a childish way. This letting go process is a powerful challenge for most parents. In learning to let go of my daughter, this famous poem by Kahlil Gibran was some help.

On Parenting

Your children are not your children.
They are the sons and daughters of Life's longing for Itself
They come through you but not from you,
And though they are with you, yet they belong not to you.

You may give them your love but not your thoughts,
For they have their own thoughts.
You may house their bodies but not their souls,
For their souls dwell in the house of tomorrow,
Which you cannot visit, not even in your dreams.

You may strive to be like them, but seek not to make them like you,
For life goes not backward nor tarries with Yesterday.
You are the bows from which your children as living arrows are sent forth.
The archer see the mark upon the path of the Infinite,
And he bends you with His might that his arrows might go swift and far.

Let your bending in the archer's hand be for gladness;
For even as He loves the arrow that flies,
So He loves also the bow that is stable.

If you think your parents might be open to these ideas, you could talk about this poem with them. If you feel they wouldn't really appreciate it, you can mentally file it away until you become a parent, and your own children are teenagers or young adults. It might help you make wiser decisions than your own parents have made.

As you get older, you will be faced with times when you feel you should do what your parents want, and other times when you feel you should follow your own heart and mind. I wish I could give you a clear-cut way to decide when to do one or the other. If you feel your parents have your best interests in mind, then the better choice would be to go with their wishes. If you feel your parents are serving their own needs, instead of yours, it is probably time to become your own parent and make your own choices.

Ideally, your parent will not seek to make you like him or her. Unfortunately, many parents do just that. A friend of my daughter's, Susan, had a mother who was constantly nagging her about her weight. Susan was attractive and not overweight. The weight issue was really the mother's problem, not the daughter's. In this example, the young adult needed to stand up for herself and go against the will of the parent, because the parent was temporarily lost in her own desires, and did not have the best interests of her daughter at heart.

Have you seen the British movie, *Billy Elliot*? At first, the father in the movie is blind to his son's need to pursue a dancing career. Although every particle of the son's being longs for this pursuit, the father is set against it. In short, the father was unable to see through his son's eyes and was lost in his own self-interest. As the movie continues, however, the father is transformed and begins to understand the son. As a result, the boy's creative genius blossoms, and the love between the father and son grows stronger. There is another inspiring movie for you to see!

For a variety of reasons, you may feel forced to totally go against the wishes of your parents to the point of being cut off from them financially as well as emotionally. If this happens, I would recommend getting the help of a counselor who you feel could give you a sense of support and direction. Colleges and churches are usually a good source for this kind of assistance. In some cases, parents of friends may also be able to help you. When you make major, life-altering decisions, especially ones that go against your parents, you want to be able to check how wise these decisions are by consulting objective and hopefully loving outside sources. You will feel more supported in what you are doing, and if you have made any unhealthy or destructive decisions, you will hopefully be led back on the right track by people with more life experience than your own.

Five

How Can I Develop a Healthy, Attractive Body?

Taking good care of your body is a vital part of showing respect for yourself. Any efforts you put into eating healthier foods and developing better physical habits will end up rewarding you in so many ways. It is simply easier to pursue all the practices discussed in the previous chapters, if you are feeling strong and energetic most of the time. Think of your body like your favorite pet. Love it and treat it with the most kindness, so it will return the same to you.

Food

There are several books about how to eat in a healthy way that I have found useful. (Please see the resource section.) A lot of what I am about to tell you is just common sense. The tricky part seems to be actually following the advice. The best way to change your eating habits is by starting to change a little bit at a time. Then don't be hard on yourself when you break your good intentions occasionally. Just keep bringing yourself back to the good habit. Eventually the new way of eating will be a part of you. For example, say you decide to stop eating so much sugar. You are doing great for three days. Then someone brings a homemade cake to your apartment, and you have a big piece. Now you're mad at yourself. Don't be! This is a part of the growth process. Growth doesn't happen in a straight line. It sort of goes in a spiral, if that makes any sense to you. You move forward, then you kind of circle backwards. Then you start moving forward again maybe for a longer period of time. Then you move a little backward again, etc…Do you understand what I mean?

So here is the eating advice in a nutshell that you will find in the books I just mentioned. First of all, eat foods that are as whole, pure and natural as possible. Good foods are fresh fruits, vegetables, whole grains, nuts, and lean meats. If possible, buy organically grown foods or naturally processed meats, so you are not eating pesticides, hormones or antibiotics. Unhealthy foods are junk foods, fried foods, processed foods, caffienated drinks, white flour, alcohol, fatty foods (like red meat and pork), and sugary foods.

I realize that temptation to eat fun, yet unhealthy foods is everywhere. It is especially difficult to avoid if you find yourself eating out with friends a lot. However, it can be done! If you really look for them, you can find healthy foods at almost any restaurant.

The best solution, of course, is to do your own grocery shopping and eat at home instead of eating out a lot. (Or if your parents do the grocery shopping, tell them about your decision to start eating healthy food.) It is easier to be disciplined about your choice of food when you are at the grocery store than when you are getting ready to eat. Go shopping when you are not that hungry. Pick out only unprocessed, fresh and natural food. Read the labels and stay away from chemicals and preservatives. Then when you are home and ready to eat, you will have only healthy foods to choose from. You will have no choice but to eat good food.

Once you begin to consciously nourish your body with healthy foods, you will begin to notice many positive changes. You will have more energy. Your complexion will be clear and shining. Your digestion will improve. You will feel stronger. You will love your new healthy and attractive body. This is another example of how a little discipline brings more freedom to your life. Start today!

Below you'll find a list of healthy foods and a sample menu. These are just a few examples to help get you started. You can also find other healthy recipes in the books listed in the resource section at the back.

Eat Some Foods from Each Category Daily:

Fresh Fruits and Vegetables:	Whole Grains:	Protein:	Drinks:
Apples	Corn Tortillas	Eggs	Herb Tea
Oranges	Corn Bread	Turkey	100% Fruit Juice
Grapes	Whole Grain Crackers	Chicken	
Bananas	Whole Grain Bread	Fish	
Apricots	Brown Rice	Lentils	
Avocados	Buckwheat or	Beans	
Broccoli	Multigrain Pancakes		
Carrots cauliflower	Popcorn		
Green beans			
Zucchini			
Tomatoes			
Lettuce (greener the better)			

Nuts and Dairy: (Just a Little)
String Cheese
Monterey Jack Cheese
Cottage Cheese
Yogurt (Plain with real fruit and honey)
Frozen Yogurt
Nuts

Sample Healthy Eating Menu

Breakfast Suggestions:

One Egg, whole wheat toast with a little butter and jam, herb tea

Old Fashioned Oatmeal (not the kind with sugar) with a little milk, fruit and cinnamon

Pancakes made with buckwheat or multi-grain flours (get a mix at grocery or health food store) with butter and syrup

Whole grain, low sugar cereal with skim milk

Fruit and Yogurt

Lunch Suggestions:

Sandwich on toasted whole grain bread with turkey, avocado, lettuce, tomato or sprouts. Substitute any lean meat. Serve with baked chips and mineral water, 100% fruit juice or herb tea (iced or hot).

Falafel on whole grain pita bread with yogurt sauce or humus. You can buy falafel or humus ready made at health food stores, like Whole Foods or HEB or make it yourself from a mix.

A big fruit salad with yogurt and honey dressing.

Leftovers from the previous night's healthy dinner.

Progresso canned soup with whole grain toast and Monterey Jack Cheese. Progresso soups come in a variety of types: lentil, split pea, chicken rice, etc...

Fried egg sandwich on whole grain toast

A big salad with some form of protein, such as chicken, turkey, cheese, tofu or almonds.

Dinner Suggestions:

Make enough to last two or three days. You can freeze it for longer.

Sautéed chicken breast with onions and Cajun spice or some spices you like. Asparagus with a little butter and Parmesan sauce and little red potatoes. (Cut chicken into fairly small pieces and sauté in olive oil with onions and spices.)

Chili with turkey meat. Read directions on prepackaged chili spice mix. Substitute turkey for beef. Serve with a big salad and corn bread.

Marinate chicken in olive oil and spices or yogurt and spices. Grill on a "lean mean grilling machine". Serve with vegetables or a salad and toast.

Mash up black beans and cook in olive oil with onion and garlic. Spread on cooked tostado shells. Garnish with salad, cheese, yogurt and picante sauce. Serve with brown rice.

Grill or bake fish or shrimp. Serve with vegetables and rice. (Use precooked fish for a faster alternative.)

Foods to Avoid

White Sugar

There are several reasons to avoid eating white, processed sugar. For one, it depresses your immune system, so it is more difficult for you to fight off sickness. When I finally stopped eating white sugar for several months, I began to notice I had more energy in general, and I was rarely sick. When I was a teenager and ate lots of sugary foods, I was almost always congested.

Have you ever noticed that when you eat white sugar, you first get a burst of energy, and then you get an energy slump afterwards? In other words, sugar is a kind of drug. It doesn't give you steady nutrition and contribute to your well being in a consistent, nurturing way.

Don't just take my word for it. Try it yourself. When you feel like eating something sweet, eat a beautiful piece of fruit. Fruit has all kinds of nutrients, fiber and natural sugar. The natural sugar in fruit is easy for your body to process. After a couple weeks of eating natural, instead of white sugar, you fill begin to notice a difference. I know you will feel better, and in the long run, your overall health will improve.

White Flour

White flour is another processed food that has very little nutritional value. Once you start paying attention to it, you will notice it is in a wide variety of foods. Cakes, cookies, white bread, pizza crust, certain crackers (Ritz, Saltines, etc.), pancakes, rolls and others. You may start thinking, "What is there left to eat?" if these have been a main stable of your diet.

Again, the idea is to eat whole grain, less processed foods. Choose bread and crackers with seeds and whole grains in them. Eat oatmeal, whole grain cereal, whole grain or buckwheat pancakes for breakfast, instead of processed cereal, white bread and white flour pancakes. Once you change this habit, you will wonder why you liked white flour foods so much. Whole grain foods really have a lot more personality and taste, and, of course, their nutritional value and fiber is far superior.

Red Meat and Pork

Red meat and pork contain large quantities of animal fat, known as lard. As you probably know, fat takes a long time to digest, is bad for your heart and produces cellulite on your body. Also, most red meat and pork often contain a lot of hormones and antibiotics that were fed to the animal. Your body will really appreciate it, if you eat chicken or fish when you are in the mood for meat. If you're feeling really courageous, try eating "Boca Burgers". They taste amazingly like hamburgers, but are made out of soybeans. My daughter eats them just like a hamburger on a bun with cheese, lettuce and tomato. Believe it or not, she actually likes them. You can also buy "Tofu Pups" which are hot dogs made from soy. I like those, but my daughter doesn't. Try eating them with some vegetarian chili sauce!

Caffeine

I know going to Starbuck's and drinking a nice Frapachino is a fun and popular pastime. And there is nothing wrong with enjoying some fun foods every once in a while. However, as you probably know, drinking caffeine is not a healthy regular habit. Just like white sugar, it is a kind of drug that gives you a temporary burst of energy and then ends up weakening your system in the long run. According to a Houston ophthalmologist, Dr. Huff, caffeine also contributes to a person's tendency to develop the eye disease, glaucoma. He told me that he has observed patients with this disease improve once they cut back on their coffee.

I have also read that caffeine has been linked to arthritis. I worked with a teacher once who had already began developing arthritis in her twenties. I asked her if she drank coffee, and she told me she started as a child and still drinks several strong cups a day. I told her about the health connection, but at the time, she was too addicted to her routine to stop.

The authors of one of my favorite and best-selling nutrition books, *Fit For Life II,* say the following about caffeine: "It takes twenty-four hours for one cup of coffee to pass through the kidneys and urinary tract. People who have several cups of coffee, chocolate, and sodas have lots of caffeine in their bloodstream. The distress and stimulation from caffeine can inhibit sleep, especially sound sleep. The body must expend energy in expelling the caffeine, plus it generates less energy at the same time because of lack of sleep, a terrible cycle. Those supposedly innocent cups of coffee during the day take their toll during the night."[1]

You might want to look into drinking herbal teas. There are so many different flavors to choose from, and some taste great with a little milk and honey. Several of them can actually cure some physical problems as well as provide you with a warm and healthy drink. You can find more information about the healing effects of herbal teas in some books listed in the back.

Alcoholic Drinks

As you know, alcohol is also a drug. People use it to slow down their thoughts and so feel a false sense of happiness or self-confidence. Everyone enjoys the temporary feelings that drugs bring, but they also are forced to experience the down side. The flip side to the good feelings varies from person to person and depends on how much you drank, what you drank, your own psychology, and other factors. If you go out and drink often, you may begin to experience symptoms such as anxiety, paranoia, increased anger, loss of memory and lack of self-control to the point of hurting yourself.

---

[1] Page 139. Harvey and Marilyn Diamond, *Fit for Life II.* New York: Warner Books, 1987.

In addition to the psychological effects, alcohol also is not good for your body. Did you know that every time you drink you kill some brain cells? Your liver is also affected by a drinking habit. Psoriasis of the liver is a disease caused by alcoholism. Alcoholic drinks are also high in calories. Wouldn't you rather spend your extra calories on one of your favorite foods?

The Greek principle of "moderation in all things" also applies to drinking. One or two casual drinks with your friends once a week or so will probably not do much harm to you. Also, take your time when you drink and sip slowly. The alcohol will have less effect if you spread the process out over time. Try to eat something before or while you drink. That will also lessen the effect of the alcohol, as will drinking a glass of water between drinks.

Foods with Lots of Additives

Get in the habit of reading labels on foods. You'll be surprised what you discover. Dunkin' Donuts' label, for example, is about a paragraph long. Those donuts are filled with all kinds of chemicals and preservatives I have never even heard of. Shipley's Donuts, on the other hand, contain no additives, and actually some healthy flours. Another example is fruit juices. Some are 100% fruit and contain only natural sugar. Others have only a small percentage of fruit juice and are packed with white sugar. It just takes a little time to make yourself aware of what you are really eating, and your body will really appreciate your extra effort.

Although I want to discourage you from eating unhealthy foods, I don't want you to feel restricted and start eating less. Most dieting is not good for you. I eat as much as I feel like, and am not overweight, simply by focusing on eating nutritious foods that I feel show respect for my body. *Once you start eating a really healthy diet, an amazing thing happens. Your cravings for sugar and other unhealthy foods begin to lessen. When your body gets the nutrition and care it has been looking for, you will feel more satisfied and less hungry. When this happens, it becomes a lot easier to continue with your new habits*

Susan S. Weed, a herbalist and nutritionist, writes: "**Frequent dieting, fasting, bingeing and purging unbalance your electrolyte levels, causing weakening of the heart muscle and damage to the heart…Eat as much as you want of whole grains, vegetables, beans, greens, fruits, fish, seeds, yogurt. Go easy on nuts, cheese, and milk. Drink water and herbal infusions as your beverages.**"[1] Think positively. Focus on what you can eat, not on what you should avoid! Make your goal self-respect and health, not thinness. I promise you your body will become stronger and trimmer without dieting if you follow these guidelines.

You can try experimenting with eating healthier foods immediately. Please do not try to change your habits all at once. Also, stay away from unbalanced diets, such as the all meat or all carbohydrate type diets. Going on an extreme diet will not help you get established in good eating habits. They are also just plain not good for you.

Eat a healthy, balanced diet and be nice to yourself by going off of it occasionally with some fun foods. The foods you love have a lot of comfort value for you. Some of them are a part of your childhood memories and may make you feel loved when you eat them. If you want to develop healthier eating habits, start changing a little at a time. You might want to try eating healthy for one day out of the week, and then eventually increase the days. Or you may want to change one habit at a time, say replacing white flour products with whole grain ones, or eating chicken and fish instead of red meat. Whatever you do, do it gradually. If you go "cold turkey" and try to change all at once, you will feel miserable and give

---

[1] Pages 181-182. Joan Borysenko, *Fire in the Soul.* New York: Warner Books., 1993.

up. Be disciplined but be very kind to yourself. Good habits take a while to develop.

(There is also another wonderful side benefit of eating a really healthy diet. If you decide to use herbs as a way of curing any physical problems you might have, a good diet is a necessity. Herbal remedies have a hard time working if your body is clogged up with a lot of toxins from unhealthy eating. The herbalist, Ed Smith writes, "Herbs by themselves can only be expected to do so much. For optimal results they should be used in the context of a natural wholesome diet, ample exercise and rest, a positive attitude, fulfilling work and a simple lifestyle. This combination will almost always have a favorable influence on one's health and often induces healing where modern medicine has failed."[2] You will find more about using herbs and other healing methods later in this chapter.)

[1].Page 139. Harvey and Marilyn Diamond. *Fit for Life II*. New York: Warner Books, 1987.

[2] Preface. Ed Smith, *Therapeutic Herb Manual*. Williams, Oregon: Ed Smith, 1999.

Eating Disorders

If you have had serious problems with eating, such as anorexia or bulimia, first know that you have a lot of company. These are very common issues among teenagers and young women today. There are some books that will shed some light for you on the cultural or psychological origins of these disorders. Check with your local bookstore or on the internet. (One suggestions is in the resource section.)

From what I have read and observed, it is my feeling that anorexia and bulimia are most fundamentally the result of young women learning to

[2] Thich Nhat Hanh, *Peace is Every Step—The Path of Mindfulness in Everyday Life*. New York: Bantam, 1992.

dislike themselves in a deep way. This is the opposite of learning to know their true Selves.

When you don't value who you really are, you often begin to abuse and disrespect yourself in various ways. Not eating or vomiting regularly is a way of hurting your body. It can be so extreme that it becomes suicide. This is a profound result of self-hatred.

On the surface, a young woman who is anorexic may feel she is simply trying to make herself more attractive so that others will admire her and love her more. Unfortunately, acquiring love in this way is an impossible dream if the young woman cannot love and admire herself in the first place. It is an essential truth that in order to receive love, we must first feel love, especially toward our own inner Self. Seeking this love by becoming thinner and thinner grows more futile and frustrating with time, and so the young woman becomes more desperate. The answer to this dilemma as is the answer to all forms of spiritual and psychological suffering is again—Learn to know and love your own Self.

Of course, this takes time. If you are struggling with an eating issue, please don't suffer alone. Psychological issues can have a way of taking on a life of their own, and helping yourself can become impossible. I would suggest finding a therapist that you really admire and feel comfortable with. And repeating what I said in another chapter, talk to several therapists, before you decide. Some can really help you, and some can't.

As you know, our popular culture (MTV, magazines, movies, etc...) bombards us with images of very thin women. The message behind these influences is that women are valued mostly for their bodies, and only for very thin bodies. I want you to know that this is a very confused way of thinking, and you can choose to not absorb it.

The message I would like you to learn is that the real you is not your body. Your body is constantly changing. Once you were in a baby's body, and in the future you will be in an old woman's body. These bodies are not *you*. You simply wear them in the same way you wear a suit of clothes. Have you ever heard accounts by people who have had near-death experiences?

They have died for a short time, and then were revived somehow. They often report the experience of floating above their body as it lies on a hospital table. When they awaken and go back to their everyday life, their whole perspective on their body has changed. They don't identify with it as strongly as they did before the near-death experience. As a result they are closer to understanding who they really are.

Even though I believe that the real me is not my body, but something deeper, I still believe in showing my body the greatest respect through eating well, exercising and having good habits. As I have said before, it is easier to follow all the spiritual practices I have talked about so far, when I am feeling strong and alert. Since I believe coming closer to knowing my Self is the purpose of my life, taking good care of my body is important to me.

Sex and Your Health

I am sure you have heard that sex can be dangerous for your health if you are not very careful about protecting yourself. If you have sex without a condom you run the risk of getting a variety of sexually transmitted diseases, including AIDS. Some of these diseases can cause you to be infertile, and, of course, AIDS could kill you, although there are some hopeful drugs available now. Some of these diseases have no symptoms, so the only way you can know if you have them is by getting tested by a doctor.

Of course, the best way to avoid these problems is to not have sex. This is the only surefire safe way. You can use a condom, and this is better than unprotected sex, but keep in mind that condoms sometimes break, and then you are again totally unprotected. Some young women think that oral sex is safe sex. This is not true. There are diseases you can get from that as well.

Reminding you of the advice about relationships that I gave you earlier in the book, if you feel you have to have sex, be sure it is with someone you trust and know very well. Before you have sex with someone, you should feel assured in every possible way that they are healthy and free of disease. This is another way for you to respect your body as well as your Self.

My daughter wanted to add a few tips here, based on her and her friends' experiences, on how to stay away from casual sex. She advises not to put yourself in situations where sex is difficult to avoid. In other words, don't let yourself be alone with a boy who is a temptation to you. Also, beware of flattery. She has noticed that boys will say anything under the sun in order to convince girls to have sex. They seem to have a special radar sometimes for knowing what girls want to hear. Flattery and expressions like "I love you" can melt a girl's heart and be very hard to resist. Also, drinking really lowers your resistance to sex. Your good resolutions may disappear after a few drinks, and when you wake up in the morning, you may wish you hadn't done what you did the night before. This is all good advice. Learn from the mistakes of others, and you'll save yourself a lot of problems!

Exercise

I am sure that you know that exercise is good for you. It builds your physical stamina and strength and helps to detoxify your system. You probably also know that it lifts your spirits by releasing natural endorphins. This is like healthy Prozac for you if you are depressed. A regular exercise program has been known to even cure depression in some cases. Remember the movie, *Forest Gump*? His natural reaction to a tragic experience was to put on his jogging shoes and start running. That was such a healthy way for him to process what happened and move ahead with his life. If you are feeling down about life, try a favorite form of exercise. Just knowing that you are getting stronger every day will also improve your mood.

A hundred years ago, exercise was more built into our everyday activities. People used their bodies more by walking, riding horses and doing chores. Now in our more mechanized society, it is easy to get into sedentary habits. We have to put some imagination into getting our bodies to move. Bodies love movement. They were built to move in order to be healthy. Without daily rigorous movement, your body will become weak and more prone to disease. Start an exercise program today!

Here's the good news. A daily exercise program really doesn't require much of your time. Just a half-hour or forty-five minutes a day is enough. Some form of aerobic exercise that makes you sweat will strengthen your heart and clear out your toxins. It will also help to tone your body as a whole.

Most gyms now offer yoga classes, if you think you would enjoy gentle stretching exercises. One of the great things about yoga is that it can really help you stay young longer. It has benefits for all the organs in your body, as well as your muscles. Older people who practice yoga have a youthful appearance due to their flexibility and lengthened spines.

If you are interested in really firming up your muscle tone, weight lifting probably brings the most dramatic results. You can join a local gym or get your own free weights. Weight lifting is a good habit to carry on as you get older if osteoporosis has been a problem among older women in your family. We tend to think of bones begin hard and unchangeable, but in reality they are a lot like muscle. Several studies have shown that weight lifting, just every other day, actually builds bone mass. If you get a regular weight lifting habit, chances are your back will remain strong throughout your life.

Exercise is one simple solution to many health problems, and in the next section I will be talking about a variety of other answers to health problems that don't involve the use of pharmaceuticals. Unfortunately, the conventional medical community often offers drugs as the solution to every problem, such as allergies, depression, impotence, menopausal issues and many others. Just watch television for a couple of hours, and you will see at least one commercial for a drug solution. However, if you take the time to look for alternative solutions, they are out there. Drug-free solutions are preferable because they usually don't come with side effects and the dangers of addiction. Be creative with your health and find the most natural and loving cures possible. There are books on a wide variety of alternative healthcare ideas that you can find at your local bookstore, health food store or on the Internet. Also, take a look at some of the magazines that suggest natural solutions to health problems. One of my favorites is *First for Women.*

Possible Solutions to Your Health Problems

Naturally if you have an extremely serious or emergency type health problem, you should see a well-qualified health professional. If you have been battling with mild, yet chronic disorders of one type or the other, the following discussion might be helpful.

Some times the solution to a health problem you might be having can be amazingly simple, just a matter of changing a habit. So first I want to focus on a few basic subjects, such as sleeping, stress and the special personality of your body.

Sleep

Some sicknesses are simply the result of not getting enough rest. You can either play or work too hard. As a result, you put extra strain on your immune system and become susceptible to germs. If you are observant, you may notice signs that you are beginning to get run done, and then reverse the process. When my daughter gets behind on her rest (usually from staying out too late too often), she begins to get congested. If she then gets extra rest, the beginning stages of a cold just go away. If she ignores the warning, she gets a really sore throat and bad cold. She ignored the warnings many times in her freshman year, and so she got sick a lot. Now that she is a junior and older and wiser, she rarely gets sick, just by paying attention to giving her body the rest it wants. Rest could be the simple solution to a variety of illnesses.

I think different bodies require different amounts of rest. Observe yourself and you will figure out how much you need. If you feel alert and rested after eight hours a night, then that is the right amount for you. Too much sleep will make you feel groggy. You may also notice when you oversleep that your dreams become weirder. This is a sign that it's time to wake up. If you sleep too much on a regular basis, it will generally weaken your body.

Too little sleep, on the other hand, will lower your immune system. If you have irregular sleep hours, as many teenagers and college students do, grab a nap when it is convenient for you. The main point is to show your body some affection by caring for it and giving it the sleep it needs. Find the perfect balance. If you listen to it, it will tell you what it wants.

Stress

Stress is another popular cause of health problems, as you are probably aware. If you notice you are under stress due to family or friend problems, school or work, take extra good care of yourself. Unfortunately, sometimes when we are stressed-out, we feel even more like eating those fun foods that we know are bad for us. We eat a box of donuts or a carton of ice cream to drown our sorrows. This just gives our poor bodies more toxins to deal with, and often the combination of stress and bad food causes us to get sick.

When you are under stress, instead of abusing your body in this way, make an effort to be extra loving to yourself. Think "I am under a lot of stress lately, what can I do for myself to balance this out?" Do something that you *really* like to do that is also good for you. Go out to lunch with a favorite friend, take a long walk with your dog, take a nap with your teddy bear, take a bubble bath with scented oil, call someone you haven't talk to in a long time, etc…Your mood will really improve just by feeling more nurtured, and you will be able to handle the stress in a lighter way.

Your Idiosyncratic Body

Everyone's body has its own unique personality. The same health rules don't apply to everyone. In Aryuvedic medicine, a 5,000 year old health philosophy from India, the doctor first discovers your mind-body type, before prescribing treatment. You can read more about their ideas in Deepak Chopra's book, *Perfect Health*.

In my case, if I eat too much sugar, I feel rundown and often get sick. If my daughter is sleep-deprived, she gets a sore throat and cold. If my husband works too many hours, he gets a headache and sinus problems. We all have our special weaknesses and strengths. I am sure you have yours. Some people are more sensitive to problems relating to food, some to exercise, sleep or stress issues. Really observe yourself and find out what kind of body you have. You will be surprised how this basic understanding of your body can cure so many of your health challenges.

Experimenting on Yourself with Natural Alternatives

When I have a health problem, I like to sort of experiment on myself with various cures. In the past thirty years, I have tried many different approaches, such as holistic medicine, Chinese herbs, homeopathy, herbal teas and tinctures and simply changing my habits based on advice from different sources. I believe in Jesus' advice, "Seek and ye shall find", and in the case of most of my health challenges, a solution eventually surfaced.

I would like to tell you about some of my adventures in healing myself as an example of the type of process you could follow when you are sick in some way. Please note that I am not saying that these solutions to specific problems will necessarily work for you. They may or they may not. It is the process of trying various things to see what works that will solve your difficulties. Also, the faith that you will find a solution will also help you.

One of my health problems when I was in my forties was that I repeatedly developed breast cysts. These are pockets of fluid in the breast that put a lot of pressure on surrounding nerves, and so hurt continuously. Two doctors told me to not eat so much salt or drink caffeine, and to take vitamin E. That wasn't the answer, because I already did those things, and it had no effect. Eventually when the pain got so unbearable, a doctor would finally drain the cyst with a syringe. This very uncomfortable situation went on for a couple of years.

I remember being in a bookstore saying a silent prayer to be shown an answer to this dilemma. I picked up a book on herbs and began reading about Nettle Leaf Tea. The author said the tea helps drain excess water out of the body. I got some, and that week, I drank several strong cups of it a day. The cysts completely disappeared! From then on I drank just one or two cups a week, and I never had this problem again.

Another chronic health problem that bothered me for more than twenty years was frequent bladder infections. When I starting having these, I would take an antibiotic. That would work great, but a few months later I would get another infection. Eventually I was getting about one every month. I felt like I was addicted to antibiotics, and that I was in poor health in general from taking them and from fighting germs off all the time. I had to really experiment a lot to find an answer to this particular health challenge. I tried drinking more water, taking more Vitamin C, drinking cranberry juice, eating a healthier diet, using certain recommended herbal teas, and doing various tests and procedures recommended by a urologist. The healthier diet improved my overall health, so I felt much stronger, but I still got a lot of infections. Finally I read something about taking the herbal tincture, Echinacea. It is an extract from a plant root, and is known to strengthen the immune system and cleanse the lympathic system. That was the answer! Since I started using it, I just had one infection, which for the first time in twenty years, actually went away without the use of antibiotics. Finally I was free from this annoying condition.

There are a few things I hope you can learn from these examples. One thing is that it you have a health problem, get advice from many sources, people and books, pray for an answer, experiment, and keep trying. I believe there is an answer to every problem. Your answers are waiting for you if you look for them. Some answers are so simple that you will be amazed. Often just changing a habit or thought pattern might help you. Get to really know your body. What works for one person may not work for another. We are all as unique as our fingerprints.

The Effect of Thought on Your Body

Christian Science is a religion that promotes healing through the use of positive thinking and understanding of spiritual truths. Thousands of Christian Scientists throughout the world have brought about personal healings, simply by changing their thought patterns, or levels of understanding. Every week in these churches, people stand up and give testimonials of how they or someone they know has benefited from the teachings.

I agree that thought and belief systems have a dramatic effect on our health. Our minds, emotions and bodies are all interconnected and work together in many mysterious ways. Whenever I am working to find a cure for one of my physical problems, I like to be open to physical as well as psychological solutions. The answer often involves a combination of so many factors.

Mind-body medicine has gained popularity in the last few years. Dr. Christiane Northrup, author of *Women's Wisdom, Women's Bodies*, discusses female problems in terms of psychological as well as physical causes. This is a great reference book for you if you have any gynecological issues. She offers countless examples of the effects of our emotions and psychology on the body. For other mind-body health books, please see the resource section.

Remember that doctors are human beings, and like all of us, they can make mistakes or lack some understanding. When you get advice from a doctor, always take it with a grain of salt. There are often many solutions to a health problem, so if you have any doubts about the doctor's suggestion, you may want to consult some other people or read up on the subject before making a decision. Doctors often play the part of imposing authority figures, so it is easy to be very influenced by them. I would like you to take your time, if possible, with any health decision and find the most loving and healthy solution for you. We no longer have to rely on conventional medical advice for our physical dilemmas. Help that is truly sympathetic to women's needs now comes from so many sources. Most of the books in the resource section can be ordered on the Internet, and some might even be at your local library.

Meditation as a Cure

As I already discussed in a previous section, meditation is the perfect tool for helping you to know your true Self. After you have practiced meditation regularly, you will really begin to enjoy the effects of deep relaxation. Your body as well as your mind will benefit. When the level of stress you carry with you is decreased by this method, related health disorders will start to disappear.

High blood pressure, anxiety, headaches and other problems are mostly caused by stress, and so when you learn how to relax deeply, these problems can become more manageable. As I mentioned earlier, the effects of regular meditation start to surprise you during the day. You will be typing on your computer or washing the dishes and the sense of "presentness" and relaxation suddenly appears. The more regularly you meditate, the more often you get these moments of focus and ease. As these moments increase, your stress symptoms begin to fade.

As you can see, good health involves a combination of several influences. I want you to learn to respect your body by feeding it nutritious food, exercising at least a half-hour a day, sleeping the right amount for you, and meditating. When you do have a health problem, first reflect on which of your habits might be the cause. If you need health advice, consider many possibilities and use your intuition. Get your answers from what you feel is the wisest and most loving source. Your body, like a much loved pet, will really appreciate all your care and attention!

Six

How Can I Stop Worrying
and Feeling Anxious?

As we discussed in the previous chapter, many women strongly identify with their bodies. It is also very tempting to identify with your brain. I grew up in a university town where education was highly valued. It seemed to me that my unspoken purpose in life was to be intelligent. I felt very pressured to get good grades and succeed as student. I couldn't even imagine doing poorly in school. Deep down I felt that if I weren't smart, I would be completely worthless. Looking back, this attitude seems crazy to me, but at the time I really believed this.

It came as a great revelation to me when I began to read about the Self. I started to understand that *I* was not my mind. My mind was really just a fancy computer for me to use when needed. The *me* that could use the computer was something altogether different. What a relief it was to finally understand this!

In this chapter I would like to help you get a good look at your mind, so you can view it with a more detached perspective. According to the spiritual teacher, Swami Muktananda, "Your mind is your heaven or your hell." Let's look into ways to live in heaven.

The Drunken Monkey

There is an eastern Indian expression that says that the mind is more difficult to subdue than a drunken monkey. Imagine a drunken monkey for a moment. Can you see him jumping all over the place, acting like a wild creature? Now try to calm him down. It's nearly impossible. Sometimes our minds are just like that. Thoughts jump from negative point to point. We worry and worry, wishing we could stop. The same song keeps playing over and over. As my daughter has said, "Sometimes I wish I could get a lobotomy!"

When your mind is agitated in this way, it is very difficult to truly experience the present moment. Instead you live in a world of thoughts, a world that can become very unreal. If your thoughts happen to be full of worry and negativity, your world can become terrifying.

Remember our discussion of mindfulness? When you are mindful, your thoughts become fewer. You feel more alive because you are more aware. You really see, hear, feel, taste and smell life. One of the reasons it can be so delightful to be around a happy child is that we begin to be in the state of mind they are in for a while. Children are naturally mindful, and their minds are fairly thought-free. Also, people like the Dalai Lama, for example, who spend their lives doing the something like the practices discussed in chapter three, develop a beautifully pure and child-like manner. This is what is known in Zen philosophy as the "beginner's mind". The mind of a child or a wise man is delightfully simple and nearly thought-free a large part of the time.

You too can learn to be the master of your mind. You really don't have to be its slave and so continually be at its mercy. If your mind is in turmoil at the moment, and you have no experience in calming it down, you are dealing with the drunken monkey. If you have a little understanding about your mind, then you have a chance to turn your mind into a friend.

Over-thinking and Worry

Don't you hate it when your thoughts begin to multiply into horrible scenarios? Maybe you have a pain in your side, for example, and you start to think, "What if I have cancer?" Then you imagine yourself in the hospital. One thought leads to another, and soon you have pictured yourself suffering in agony and finally dying.

Or maybe you see your boyfriend talking to one of your friends. You begin to think he likes her more than you. This leads to thinking he's going to break up with you. Gradually your mind begins to fill you with dread that you will be alone, and no boy will ever like you again.

You may have some thought patterns that repeat almost every day with no outside inspiration to get them going. You may think, "I hate my hair. I'm so fat. The reason boys don't like me is that I have a big ears, etc..." These perpetual negative thoughts really chip away at your self-love and self-respect. In almost no time at all you can make yourself feel worthless.

I am sure you can think of scores of other examples of how your mind works. One thought continually gives birth to another, until you have a whole extended family of thoughts. These thoughts create the world you live in. Would you rather live in a room filled with cobwebs and frightening monsters or in a beautiful meadow of flowers and sunshine? So what is the solution?

Watching Your Thoughts

The first step is to watch your mind. It sounds so simple, but watching your thoughts as if from a distance is a very powerful thing to do. Can you see what you are thinking right now? When you watch your thinking from a place deep inside yourself, slowly the thoughts begin to lose their force. You begin to see, "Look, there I go again with that thought pattern. It's that same old one again." Once you can do that, you have gained what is called "detachment". You see your thoughts as simply thoughts, not as an integral part of who you are.

After you have played around with watching your thoughts for a while, you can try this experiment. Make yourself think five or more positive thoughts. They could be anything that is cheerful and inspiring. It could be: "Great—tomorrow is Saturday. It's almost summer. I might get a new job. I loved that joke I just heard." You will notice something incredible. No matter how bad your mood was, it will have just improved by this simple exercise. Hopefully, this will convince you how much your thought influences your feelings and how you have the power to change those thoughts. **If you really understand this, you can improve your whole life!**

I do this little practice several times every day. It seems so simple, but it really contributes to my cheerful state of mind. I have been writing this chapter for about an hour, and I just became a little tired of writing. I decided to take a break. I got myself a snack and sat spaced-out at my desk, creating a few fun thoughts. Instantly, my cranky, down feeling was transformed, and I felt refreshed. This habit is one of the many ways I have found to be good to myself.

There is another result of learning to watch your own thoughts. You can also become aware of who is watching the thoughts. Try this. Watch your thoughts for awhile. See them clearly. Now notice, who is watching the thoughts. What is it that is not thinking, but is just aware and watching? In eastern philosophy, this is known as the Witness. In other words, it is the part of you that is aware and is not thinking or feeling. As you probably know by now, that is your inner Self. You have just glimpsed that part of yourself that never changes, the part that is always with you as your constant companion. Jesus and Buddha lived in this awareness continuously, and this is why people were healed and felt so much love around them.

Pulling Out Weeds

Picture yourself in a garden. It is overgrown with all kinds of weeds and vines. You want to turn this space into a beautiful setting that you and everyone else can enjoy. Your first step is to pull out all the weeds. You make sure you get the roots too, so they won't keep growing back. You buy some beautiful flowers and plant them lovingly. Your daily care of these new plants helps them flourish. Soon you have a magical place filled with beautiful colors and fragrances!

Your mind is just like this garden of yours. Once you have practiced watching your thoughts for a while, you can begin to notice which thoughts lift you up and which ones bring you down. When you notice a thought that seems to weigh a lot, you pull it out, just like a weed, and replace it with a new, brighter thought. For example, you think, "Oh no, it's time for math class. That teacher is so boring. Sigh. I don't think I can take another one of those classes." You watch your mind thinking this. Then you think, "Boy, that was a depressing thought. What can I replace that with?" Think creatively. You might be surprised by what you come up with. It could be something like, "I'm glad my chair in that class is in the sun. It's so cold today. That will really warm me up." Or you might think, "I really had a good time talking with that new student yesterday. Maybe I'll see him again." Do you get the idea? I'm not suggesting lying to yourself in any way, making up goody-goody fake positive thoughts you don't really believe in. Be creative, but be honest with yourself too.

You will find that the more you are able to do this, the better you will feel. When you share your lighter thoughts with other people, they will feel uplifted too. After you do this practice for a while, you will begin to notice your friend's comments as well. If you have a friend whose comments are always depressed or bitter, you might want to talk to them about it. Tell them what you read, and what you are trying to practice. If you are struggling to really change and be more positive, the impact of the people around you on your mood is very important. Start to be aware of who you choose as friends. Find friends that help you move closer to knowing the beautiful garden that exists inside of you. Resist friends that keep filling your garden with weeds and annoying insects.

Think Less Thoughts

After you have developed some ability watching and replacing thoughts, you can try this practice. Think fewer thoughts. You will be surprised how good this feels. If your mind is continually filled with heavy thoughts, the thoughts are very dense, and it will be difficult to think less. They are sort of like heavy furniture. It's nearly impossible to move them around. However, once you begin to think lighter, more cheerful thoughts, you will find you magically have more power to think less. And when you think less, you instantly feel happier.

As we have already discussed, there are some tools you can use to help you think less. One is being mindful, just focusing on doing one thing at a time with your total attention. And the other is meditation, clearing your thoughts out by repeatedly returning your focus to a mantra of some kind. Even if you haven't started doing these exercises, but are simply practicing watching and replacing thoughts, you can begin to think less just by making an effort to do so.

Of course, some thinking is good. You need to think to pass a test or answer your friend's question or decide where you want to go on vacation, etc…However, you don't need to think the same thoughts over and over, especially self-destructive thoughts. Once you begin to watch your mind, you will be astounded at how much unnecessary thinking you do. It's really a waste of energy.

When I began to practice watching my mind and thinking less, I had the wonderful feeling that my life became simpler. Every activity I do now seems easier. I seem to get dinner cooked effortlessly, when I am not thinking so much. I get myself ready for work without that old sense of dread. Life seems more to happen by itself without my trying to control it. Life really isn't simpler now. I probably get more done now than I did before. *It just feels simpler.*

Feeling, Expressing and Watching Emotions

Human beings feel all kinds of emotions: fear, anger, love and joy, to name the most basic ones. One valuable thing to know about emotions is that they are like waves in the ocean—they come in and they go out. If you feel overcome by, say, anger, and you really don't want to say or do something you will regret, simply wait a couple of minutes. Stop yourself from doing or saying anything until the wave of anger passes. This is why it is often suggested to count to ten. It allows some time for the wave to begin to go out. If you can do this, you have a lot of personal power over your emotions.

Some people say you should always express your feelings. They feel it is unhealthy to keep things locked inside. This modern philosophy has some truth to it, but it is not the complete picture. I believe it is good for you to feel all your feelings and to find out what messages they are trying to give you. **Ideally, whether you express them or not is a choice you make from a centered place inside yourself.**

I once heard a story about a psychologist who often preached the concept of emotional self-expression. One day while he was lecturing, a man ran up to him out of the audience and expressed his emotion by punching the poor psychologist in the face. I'm sure that experience changed the therapist's philosophy very quickly.

When you have a strong feeling about something, feel it. Watch it. Listen to it. You can be sure it is there for a reason. All feelings have a purpose and a message for you. Never think, "I shouldn't be having this feeling. I'm a bad person for feeling this way." **Feelings are very real. You cannot help what you feel.** They are like an e-mail from a friend. It's just a message. You are not good or bad for receiving the message. You just need to read it. Then you can decide whether you want to do anything about it.

When I was a little girl, I remember feeling bad about a lot of my feelings. I felt guilty that I was angry with my mother. I was confused about why I felt lonely around my family. I was mystified by feelings of anxiety. I didn't understand that these feelings were a natural result of the life I was living. It really made perfect sense for me to be feeling what I was feeling. Since I spent a lot of energy, trying to pretend I didn't have these negative feelings, I felt some inner conflict along with the emotion. Of course, this made my life at the time more difficult.

Fortunately, when I grew up I was able to take another look at my childhood feelings from a wiser and healthier viewpoint. With the help of a therapist, I re-experienced different parts of my childhood and this time, when I felt something, I listened to it. I began to understand there were lots of reasons I had been angry with my mother. I had felt lonely because people in my family were mostly absent, either physically or in other ways. I had been anxious because my contact with my emotions and my inner Self was constantly stifled. I slowly began to realize that all of my feelings made perfect sense. Once I figured this out, I began to feel more real.

When you feel something, really take a look at what that feeling is trying to teach you. If you feel nervous, think about what you are afraid of. If you feel jealous, find out if there is some way that you can develop what the person you are jealous of has or maybe just feel grateful for what you do have. If you are angry, discover what action you should take or what change of attitude you may need. Every feeling you have is there for a reason. Listening to your feelings can teach you a lot about yourself and really help you evolve to a higher level.

After you have listened to the meaning behind the feeling, the next step is to decide if you want to express that feeling or not. If your friend makes you angry, do you really want to slap her across the face? If you like a boy and feel a sudden burst of affection, do you want to run up to him and hug him? If you feel sad in the middle of class, should you start crying?

Naturally sometimes you may be overcome by emotion, and you feel as if you have to express those feelings. In these cases, you may have no choice. At other times, you may have a little distance from your feelings, and you have the sense that you can watch what you are feeling. This situation gives you a little more power and strength of character. Then you can decide in a wiser way what you want to do with the feeling.

This is where dharma comes in again. Do you remember that discussion? When you make a dharmic decision, you move closer to being in touch with your inner Self. As Jesus would say, you are following God's will. The more dharmic your life becomes, the more your "circle of compassion" expands, and you feel more connection to the people around you. When you are deciding whether to act on an emotion or not, think whether the action will bring positive results to you and others. Will it help you expand and progress, or take you backwards? Will love or hatred increase?

If your friend makes you angry, probably slapping her won't help either one of you in the long run. Getting away from the friend, cooling down and later talking with her about what happened would probably bring better consequences. If you are feeling affectionate around a boy, in certain circumstances, hugging him would bring you both a sense of love and connection. In other instances, you might scare the boy away with an unexpected burst of enthusiasm. Whether it is dharmic to cry in class or not, would also depend on the circumstance. In some instances, you would change the whole atmosphere of the classroom and illicit sympathy and caring from everyone around you. In other cases, you might be just annoying people by trying to get attention. Deciding whether to act on a feeling or not, requires you to look deep inside yourself and consider what would be the best choice for you and others. Try asking yourself, if a wise person, like Jesus or the Dalai Lama, were with me, what would he suggest?

Often people are leaning too much one way or the other. Some people feel they have to express every feeling that they have. This usually ends up getting them in a lot of trouble. I am sure you know people who are always exploding into anger or bursting into tears. It is very challenging for them to establish harmonious relationships with all this emotional activity going on all the time. Other people are too self-controlled. I was one of those for the first half of my life. I had trouble feeling and expressing most emotions, and this gave me a feeling of isolation from my Self and most people.

Of course, the answer is to find a middle ground. Feel your feelings, and listen to their messages. Express them when you feel it will help you move forward. If you don't want to express them, take some time to work with them. You could write about them in your journal, contemplate them, discuss them with your friends. There are many things to do with feelings besides acting on them. Just because you don't express feelings, doesn't mean you are repressed. As long as you feel them and learn from them, you are probably in pretty good mental health.

Feeling Depressed and Anxious

When a young woman is depressed, she often feels a sense of emptiness as well as having some feelings of anxiety at times. She may feel like life has no meaning or point to it, that she is just going through the motions of living for no reason. She may feel very little enthusiasm for anything. She may feel like sleeping or eating a lot. Or she may have the opposite reaction and have trouble sleeping and no interest in food.

I remember being depressed my last semester of college. I could sleep all right, but had to make myself eat. It was a tremendous amount of work, since I simply had no appetite. I felt a constant sense of fear in the pit of my stomach. It sort of felt like I was treading water to just stay alive. At the time, I didn't understand why I was experiencing all this.

Although we use the phrase, "*feeling* depressed", depression is really the absence of feeling, more than a feeling itself. Depression is the result of being out of contact with who we really are. For one reason or another, we have stopped feeling our normal range of feelings. So the first step in helping yourself, is to discover what feelings you are denying.

Is there something going on in your life that really makes you sad? Do you need a really good cry? Or is there something that is making you very angry, but for some reason, you feel you shouldn't be angry? Is there some action you need to take, but you feel frozen and can't take it? Once you get at what you are really feeling, you need to work with it in the ways we have discussed already. If you can't figure out what feelings you have buried, then you need the help of a therapist. Sometimes buried feelings go way back to your childhood experiences, and your present life experience is beginning to dig them up.

In my situation that last semester of college, I had buried a whole truckload of feelings. A more emotionally healthy person would have been experiencing a lot of feelings, but I was so used to denying feelings that I felt nothing. My father died, I was breaking up with my boyfriend, and I was about to leave school and start a new life. I should have been feeling sadness, regrets, loneliness, fear and other emotional messages. Instead by blocking all the vitality of my feelings, I became sort of half-dead.

If you are experiencing depression, know that you are not alone in this. Depression is far more common in women than it is in men, and it is especially common at your time of life. If you go to a therapist for help, try to stay away from anti-depressant drugs (unless you are very suicidal). You need to become more alive to cure your depression, not more drugged. You need to feel, to listen and probably to act. Taking drugs is only a temporary fix, and latter you will have to deal with breaking a dependence on them.

Don't worry that depression will hurt you. Even though your stomach hurts and your heartbeats fast, it won't damage you. You are young, and your body can tolerate a lot. I remember I used to worry I would have a heart attack when my heart would beat fast from anxiety, but my basic health was always okay. You will be all right. Once you discover what Life is trying to communicate to you, these bad feelings will go away, and you will be a wiser and more compassionate person as a result of this experience.

There are two main points to this chapter that I want to underscore. The first is that when you learn to work with your thoughts (in the ways described), you will lighter, freer and happier in general. Your relationship with yourself and others will become more loving. Life, in general, will just seem simpler. The other point is that your emotions are very valuable messages for you in your quest to know your true Self. Really respect and listen to them, but don't always act on them. Find a happy medium between emotional self-control and self-expression, and you will live a more balanced and harmonious life.

In the next chapter, we'll take a look at your dreams. This is one of my favorite subjects! I hope you enjoy the following discussion.

Seven

What do My Dreams Mean?

Dreams are a significant part of your inner life. Even though you may not remember your dreams, you really do dream every night. Studies have shown that rapid eye movement always accompanies dream activity, and that people experience this type of movement several times during every sleep. If you don't remember any of your dreams, there are a few easy things you can do in order to become more aware of them.

The first is just to resolve that you will pay more attention to your dreams. Just this simple resolution will start the process happening. Whenever you wake up in the middle of the night or in the morning, notice if you were dreaming. If you remember anything at all, review it in your mind several times, so you could tell the story to someone else. You could also keep a small notebook by your bed and write down the dream. If you have not paid much attention to your dreams before, be patient. You may remember one dream on one night and then nothing for several. However, I can promise you that the more you focus on noticing and remembering, the more your dreams will begin to talk to you.

My husband used to barely remember any dreams that he had. I was very interested in my dream-life, so when my daughter was little, I would always talk to her about her and my dreams. It became a part of our family discussions, so slowly, my husband began to pay more attention to his dreams, and they have remained the source of many interesting stories and ideas.

What is the purpose of dreams?

I believe that dreams are messages from you inner Self. They can warn you when you are off-balance in your life in some way. They can make you aware of a feeling you may be denying. They can also change an attitude you have that needs adjustment in order for you to lead a happier life. (Remember the effect of Scrooge's dream in *The Christmas Carol* or Nicolas Cage's dream in *The Family Man?*) Some dreams may even predict events for you. Dreams are very powerful and mysterious and have so much valuable information to communicate to you.

How do I interpret my dreams?

As you know, most dreams come to you in a symbolic form, so to understand what they are saying, you need to learn how to interpret them. The more you practice interpreting them, the better you will get.

First, notice what you were feeling in the dream. Just like in real life, a feeling carries an important message for you. If you have a lot of dreams in which you feel afraid or even terrified, it's a safe bet that there is something in your present life that presents a danger to you. Find out what it is. If your dreams seem to have an anger theme, there is probably some action you need to take. The emotion behind the dream can be one of the most important messages.

When you are looking at the plot of the dream, try this approach. Whether you are aware of it or not, you have many different personalities inside of yourself. Some parts of you are like your family members, your friends or your enemies. Imagine each of the characters in your dreams is one of your own personalities or some aspect of your inner life. What is that part trying to tell you? In the following dream examples, you can get a better idea of how this type of interpretation works.

From what I have read and experienced, there are many types of dreams. The most basic ones that I discuss here are message, prediction, wish fulfillment and communications with people who have died.

Message Dreams

Message dreams are dreams that have something to tell you about your present life. They may warn you of something you are not seeing so clearly, point out an emotion you may be denying, or clarify the meaning behind something you are experiencing. The snake and alligator dream is a good example of this type of dream. It also makes a prediction.

The Snakes and Alligators Dream

A few months ago a friend of mine dreamt that she and her daughter were swimming together towards a river. They looked down in the river, and it was filled with huge snakes and alligators. She told her daughter they should just stay close to the top of the water, and hopefully the creatures wouldn't notice or hurt them. They swam cautiously on and made it safely to the big lake, where they were safe.

At the time of this dream the daughter had been worried she might be pregnant. She had had several dangerous experiences with boys. The mother, of course, was also worried about her daughter's lifestyle, and that she might be pregnant. After the dream, she told her daughter she thought it meant they had been swimming in dangerous waters, but would come out of it all safely. This really comforted the daughter, and a few days later she found out she wasn't pregnant.

Interpreting this dream was fairly simple. The main feelings were fear and then a sense of relief and safety. The inner Self was showing the mother a glimpse of the future, and illustrating the conditions of her daughter's life in a symbolic form. It was helpful to both of them to share this story, which so imaginatively and simply summed up one of their present life challenges. It was also a source of encouragement.

The Guru and the Elevator Dream

I once dreamt I was waiting for an elevator with the spiritual master named Gurumayi and a group of her followers. Everyone, including myself, was so excited that we would get to ride in an elevator with this magical person. I was smiling and feeling great, as were the others. The elevator was supposed to go up. Suddenly a woman came up to me and was chattering away. She said we had to take the escalator down to the basement and look at some clothes. I felt so irritated to be taken away from this happy situation. I thought, "I don't even know what she's talking about!"

When I was thinking of this dream, I first looked at the predominant emotions, happiness and irritation. Then I thought of each of the characters in the dream as some aspect of myself. The guru was my true Self, the people were the part of me that loves the inner Self, and the annoying, chattering lady was my own thoughts when they keep talking inside my head.

The dream showed me how the parts of my inner world were working together at that time. Clearly, I had a desire to be near my true Self and even go up to a higher level through being in contact with the Self. However, my overactive mind kept getting in the way, and was literally bringing me down. I liked the dream because it gave me a clear illustration of what was going on with me.

Sometimes I like to imagine the dream situation but rewrite it in a hopeful way. I imagine I say goodbye to the annoying lady, and take a wonderful trip in the elevator with this spiritual master, absorbing her sense of love and bliss the entire time.

You too can do this with any of your dreams when you wake up. It is sort of like rewriting your childhood experiences. If your dream has an unhappy ending, change it to a more positive one. If you are feeling afraid, give yourself more power in the dreams and conquer the situation. If you are angry in the dream, take whatever action is necessary to resolve the conflict positively.

Prediction Dreams

I believe your inner Self knows a lot about the future. Sometimes it will let you in on what it knows. Some people seem to have a knack for this kind of dream. I think that the more we pay attention to our dreams, the more likely this kind of dream becomes. Be careful though. You may think a dream is predicting the future, and it may only be showing you what will happen if you continue on your present course. It may be trying to steer you away from something. Think of Scrooge's dream in *The Christmas Carol.* The ghost of Christmas Future painted a horrible picture for him of what his life would be like if he continued in his state of mind. He and everyone around him suffered in someway. This wasn't a prediction, but a warning. Sometimes it's challenging to know the difference. The following is an example of one of my husband's dreams. His dreams are usually simple and to the point.

The Bankruptcy Dream

My husband woke up startled one morning and said he had just dreamt that his medical supply company went bankrupt. I asked him if he thought this was true, and he said it was likely that it was on its last legs.

He went to the morning meeting and found out that due to several circumstances, it really was losing lots of money. At this point he decided to sell it. In other similar circumstances, he had worked to pull the company up with outside investments, but now the time had arrive to call it a day.

The dream was helpful in that it prepared him to meet that morning's news without surprise. The dream showed him things to come and helped him decide how to handle the situation before he was in it.

The Man on a Tightrope Dream

Several months before I met my husband I had the following dream. In the dream a dark-skinned man was walking over an ocean on a tightrope.

I thought he came from far away. I also thought he was such a balanced person (as the tightrope seemed to symbolize). I knew there was something special about this man. The dream impressed me enough so that I remembered it for a long time.

When I met my husband, the dream made sense, and I realized it had been a prediction. My husband came from India, was dark-skinned, and I felt he was a well-balanced person. It seemed so magical that my inner Self knew he was coming into my life before I even met him.

Wish Fulfillment

This is a very common type of dream and usually very pleasurable. These dreams offer us experiences we can't have in our everyday life for one reason or another. They sort of fill in something we are missing at the time. This kind of fantasy helps to make us feel more balanced instead of frustrated by the continuous longing for things we can't have. These kinds of dreams, I feel, are very good for our overall mental health. Enjoy these dreams when you have them!

The Desserts and Boys Dream

My daughter had the following wish fulfillment dream. She dreamt she went to a party at someone's apartment. There were all kinds of different cakes and pastries for refreshments. She went around trying different ones. All the boys at the party liked her and were paying her lots of attention. She felt very happy.

This dream came during a time of her life when she was really watching what she ate and working to get into healthier eating habits. Obviously, she was really missing eating desserts. Also, she really wanted a boyfriend. The dream gave her a refreshing break from the two frustrations she had been experiencing.

Vacation Dreams

I have had several dreams that I am on vacation. I feel very light-hearted and relaxed. I enjoy shopping in little stores, walking on a beach, going swimming and other vacation-type things.

I think these dreams may be designed to balance out my common feeling that I have a lot of work to do. The dreams show me a state of mind that is opposed to the pressured, over-organized attitude that I often find myself feeling.

Communications

It is very common to dream about people who have died. Sometimes there are issues we want to continue working on with that person. Dreaming about these feelings helps us to resolve them without the person actually being with us. I have had many dreams about my mother, since my relationship with her was probably the most challenging one of my life. In the dreams I experience many of the same old feelings I had when she was alive. When I wake up, I often like to rewrite the dream in my head and make the situation less uncomfortable and more harmonious. I feel these dreams help me work through some old negative impressions.

I also believe that sometimes in very special dreams we can actually communicate with someone who is on a different level of reality. My husband's sister died when they were both teenagers, and he often felt she was really talking to him when he dreamed about her. I have read other accounts of people who had the same impression. These dreams usually feel very real, more real than the usual types of dream.

My Husband Meets My Father Dream

One night after we had attended a family reunion, my husband had the following dream. He saw a big white house with many rooms in it. He began walking around all the empty rooms and came to one where he saw my father. My father introduced himself. He said he was happy to meet my husband and shook his hand. He also told my husband to take good care of Joanie (me). When my husband woke up, he felt as if it had been a real experience.

In the Bible, Jesus describes another plane of reality by saying, "My father has many rooms." My husband felt this dream image of a white house with many rooms symbolized this other plane or heaven. When he told me the dream, I cried because the dream gave me such a sense that my father was protecting me, even though he died many years ago.

I would like to offer you one warning about dream interpretation. Beware of dream books that list symbols and pat explanations for what dream symbols mean. Symbols in your dreams are designed especially for you. If you love cats, a cat appearing in your dream will mean something different to you that to someone who has had traumatic experiences with cats. Symbols come from your past experiences. They derive their meaning from the meaning they have in your life. If you are working to figure out what something in your dream symbolizes, think about that thing and notice all the associations you have with it. Also, notice how you feel about that thing, person or situation. This will give you so many clues about what that part of your dream symbolizes.

When you begin to take regular notice of your dreams, see if they fall into any of these categories. You may even come up with some dream types of your own. Dreams are like stories written just for you. Once you make them a part of your everyday life, you will begin to feel like you and your inner self have a fascinating conversation going on. Enjoy sharing your dreams with your friends. Dreams often make very colorful stories! If you want to read more about dream interpretation, see the resource section for a book suggestion.

Eight

You are Never Alone

"*There are more things in heaven and earth...than are dreamt of in your philosophy.*"

—Shakespeare's *Hamlet*

As Einstein said in the quotation at the beginning of the book, being separate and cut off from life is really a sort of "optical delusion". In other words, it is not true. However, all of us have times when we feel lonely. You can feel lonely by yourself in your room or in a huge crowd of people. You could even feel lonely while talking to a good friend or at a family gathering. All that it takes to feel this way is a certain state of mind. Once you are in this state of confusion, loneliness becomes your only companion, and it can be difficult to shake off.

In this chapter I would like to talk to you about a few ideas that have convinced me that I am never alone. As Einstein said, feeling separate can become a lot like being in prison. Hopefully, some of these concepts will help you break free when the loneliness mood strikes.

Remember Your Inner Self

When you feel lonely, remember that you have a friend who is always with you. This is, of course, your inner Self. When Jesus said, "Fear not. I am always with you", he was hoping to reassure his disciples that they were never alone. As long as they remembered him in their hearts, his presence was there with them. Jesus, and other "realized beings", have identified themselves with the inner Self or with God. They are always with you because your inner Self is always with you. It is the same thing. All you have to do is remember that it is there.

I think it really helps if you can also imagine the presence of a person who you feel is a God-realized being. This could be Jesus, Buddha or a spiritual master whose teachings have inspired you. (There are several book suggestions in the back of the book by a variety of spiritual masters.) Imagine that great being is sitting in your room, shining with love and a feeling of total happiness. Just being around a person like that would make you feel safe and loved. It would be like being around the ideal mother or father. You would feel just like a well-protected child. You can imagine this person is with you when you are alone or in a crowd. Don't think this is a psychotic thing to do. It is a very common spiritual practice. This is one reason Jesus told his followers to think of bread and wine as his body and blood. Jesus wanted them to feel he was with them every day. Wouldn't that be wonderful to have such a wise, affectionate friend around you all the time? If you did, you would never feel alone.

Angels

Do you believe in angels? Have you ever had an angel experience? I once took a philosophy course at a catholic university, and the professor told the class that everyone had their own personal angel. I really admired him for making such a courageous statement. I'm sure a lot of the students thought he was really living in fantasyland.

As you have probably figured out, I believe that angels actually do exist. Although I have never had a direct angel experience, my husband and some of my friends have. If you would like to read some people's testimonials about angels, see the resource section for a book suggestion. Just to get you interested in the subject, here's a story one of my friends told me many years ago. My husband and I both felt honored to hear the story at the time because Karen had shared it only with a few close friends who she felt could understand. At the time, she was somewhat mystified by it herself and really was looking for an explanation.

The experience happened when she was in college. She had been going through a rough emotional time, having just broken up with her boyfriend. She was having trouble in school, and, for several others reasons, life just seemed to not be going her way. One afternoon she was lying on her bed and a person entered her room quietly. She felt afraid but couldn't move. He came over to her and placed his hand on her forehead for a moment. Then he left the room. She knows she wasn't dreaming. The experience was totally real. This moment was a turning point. Most of the struggles she was experiencing resolved themselves in the next few days.

Although this experience somewhat frightened her because she had not believed in such things before, it also gave her the sensation that she was cared for and protected. Even if you have never had an angel experience or known anyone who has, I believe you are also watched over. Just because you have never seen something doesn't mean it isn't true. Be open to the possibility.

Prayers Really Work

Many people have been taught to pray in church or when they go to bed, but they don't really believe it does much good. I never really thought much about prayer until I had a few convincing experiences and read some things about it. Now I believe that prayers, when they are truly heartfelt, can be a very powerful force. Also, the act of praying is yet another way for you to feel more connection to the universe.

A doctor named Randolph Byrd conducted a clinical study on the effects of prayer when he was working at San Francisco General Hospital. This study, which was published in the *Southern Medical Journal* in 1988, proved that prayer helped patients with heart attacks to recover. Dr. Byrd randomly assigned more than 400 patients admitted to the coronary intensive care unit with heart attacks to either standard medical care or standard care plus prayer from a distance through prayer groups. Neither the patients nor the staff knew who was being prayed for, eliminating the possibility that the prayed-for patients might get preferential treatment or heal through the placebo effect. Those who were prayed for had fewer cardiac arrests, were less likely to need mechanical ventilation, had a much-reduced incidence of pulmonary edema, suffered fewer infections and needed less medication. Without doubt, many of the patients in the control group were also being prayed for, but those in the prayer group got an extra amount of attention.[1]

I hope this study convinces you that when you pray for other people, they can really feel it physically and are greatly benefited. Make it a habit, perhaps before falling asleep, to wish all your friends and family the best of everything in your prayers. Who knows what wonderful effects will follow!

And please remember to pray for yourself as well. Any of the new positive habits you are trying to establish in your life could really use a boost of encouragement. By praying for more self-discipline, more inner strength, more love and compassionate for others, you will end up helping yourself move in the right direction, and that will in turn help others.

Aside from praying for others and ourselves, it also feels good to pray in a way that helps us feel closer to the Self or God. Meditation, as discussed at the beginning of this book, helps you clear your mind, and so begin to feel the peacefulness of the inner Self. A simple prayer, such as the following one from the Unity Church, when recited regularly and mindfully, can also help you feel less alone, and more loved and protected. If you like this little prayer, memorize it and say it to yourself a few times whenever you feel you need some sense of protection or love. You could say it inwardly if you come across a hostile person, or you are simply feeling lonely.

[1.] Pages 181-182. Joan Borysenko, *Fire in the Soul.* New York: Warner Books, 1993.

The Light of God surrounds us
The Love of God enfolds us
The Power of God protects us
The Presence of God watches over us.
Wherever we are, God is
And all is well.

The Universe Knows You Well

Now I am going to ask you to stretch your imagination even a little farther than before. Wouldn't it be amazing if there was an exact description of your personality, your strengths and weaknesses, your health tendencies, and your abilities and talents written directly by the universe? I believe there really is.

C. J. Jung, the renowned psychologist, devised the concept known as "synchronicity." He believed that sometimes two events happen at the same time that sort of mirror each other. When you were born, for example, the position of the planets formed a map of your life and inner workings. The two things, your birth and the particular map of the stars and planets, happened at the same time. If everyone could read their map easily, we would all believe that these maps are meaningful. The tricky part is interpreting the map. This is where a skillful astrological comes in. I realize these are mystifying ideas that may be hard to swallow, but try to stay with me.

C.J. Jung himself had the ability to read astrological charts, and he was a great believer in their truth. One time someone gave him around 200 unnamed astrological charts of Jung's own clients, asking him to match the charts to the names. He was able to do this with 100 percent accuracy! If the position of the planets bore no relationship to the clients' personalities, this would have been impossible.

When I first had my birth chart read by a talented astrologer who had never met me, I was astounded. It was the most detailed and accurate description of my personality and abilities anyone had ever given me. I was deeply moved by the sense that the universe really knew who I was. I felt a part of everything. I could see my life was not just an arbitrary thing, but had a plan to it. It really made me want to know more.

I began studying astrology on my own, and with the help of computer software to make the astronomical calculations, I have read several of my friends' charts. In almost every case, the person whose chart I read, felt an incredible sense of being known, not by me, who was only reading the map, but by the sky and the author of that sky. Wouldn't you love to feel that God knows you in such a personal way?

Astrology was a well-respected science in ancient times. The three kings followed astrological calculations to predict the birth of Christ. Unfortunately, now astrology has been downgraded to a New Age trend. People practice it the shortcut way by reading paragraphs in the newspaper or analyzing personality traits just by the sun sign. When these methods prove inaccurate, astrology is condemned as flaky hippie nonsense.

Astrology is a complex science that requires years of study to even scratch the surface. This is why if you decide to get your birth chart read, you should only go to someone who is highly skilled, has spent many years practicing, and has a good reputation. I know it will give you a lot of valuable information about yourself and maybe even a new sense of direction. Be adventurous!

All Things Are Connected

The following quotation was written by Thich Nhat Hanh, a Vietnamese monk who was nominated for the Noble Peace Prize. It is such a simple and wonderful description of how all things in life are connected. As Einstein said, our feeling of separateness or aloneness is really a kind of "optical delusion". It is not the truth. We just have been conditioned to look at life that way. Really consider the following thoughts. You will begin to look at a simple piece of paper in a whole new way!

"If you are a poet, you will see clearly that there is a cloud floating in this sheet of paper. Without a cloud there will be no water: without water, the trees cannot grow; and without trees, you cannot make paper. So the cloud is in here. The existence of this page is dependent on the existence of a cloud. Paper and cloud are so close.

"Let us thing of other things, like sunshine. Sunshine is very important because the forest cannot grow without sunshine, and we humans cannot grow with sunshine. So the logger needs sunshine in order to cut the tree, and the tree needs sunshine in order to be a tree. Therefore you can see sunshine in this sheet of paper.

"And if you look more deeply, with the eyes of a bodhisattva, with the eyes of those who are awake, you see not only the cloud and the sunshine in it, but that everything is here: The wheat that became the bread for the logger to eat, the logger's father—everything is in this sheet of paper."[2]

Do you see how all of life is in this one piece of paper? Isn't that an amazing idea to consider? Can you imagine that all of life is in everything? Think about it.

Start to Believe

Did you ever see the Christmas movie, *Miracle on 34th Street*? At the end of the movie, the little girl (Natalie Wood) is trying to believe in Santa Claus, but it is very difficult for her after years of being taught how to be "rational-minded". She says over and over to herself, sighing, "I believe. I believe. It's silly, but I believe." I know that if you haven't been exposed to a lot of the concepts in this book before, you may feel just like her. You would like to have some faith, but some things just don't seem real to you. That's all right. I was just like you.

---

[2] Thich Nhat Hanh, *Peace is Every Step—The Path of Mindfulness in Everyday Life.* New York: Bantam, 1992.

When I was a teenager, I didn't believe in God, angels, astrology, spiritual masters, the inner Self, and a lot of other things. Gradually, it grew on me. Just the fact that you are reading this book, and you made it all the way to the end, tells me a lot. You are beginning to open to a new world of possibilities and ideas. You are starting to develop your whole belief system. I wish you the very best on this journey inside your Self. I hope that everyday you do a little better at respecting your body, your mind and your soul. I pray that gradually your inner Self becomes your constant companion, and you are filled with more love and true joy. If you have any comments or questions, please feel free to write to me at my e-mail (*joanmishra@hotmail.com*). I've really enjoyed talking to you.

About the Author

Joan Mishra holds a bachelor's degree in English Literature from the University of Michigan with a additional major in music from St. Thomas University and a master's degree in Education from Boston University. She has over twenty-five years of experience teaching English, music, languages, and other subjects to students of all age levels. Most recently, she became the founder and director of Allegro Conservatory, an innovative preschool with a musical emphasis. Her book, *Your Preschooler Discovers the Fine Arts—An Integrative Program that Nurtures the Whole Child,* is a valuable resource for parents and teachers hoping to educate young children in a humanistic and imaginative way.

The author grew especially aware of the problems of modern young women through working with students at a junior college and from experiences with her own teenage daughter and her friends. She felt their intense need for essential answers to psychological dilemmas, and hoped that her own lifelong study of the teachings of spiritual masters and sages might provide these young women with some comfort and direction.

Resources

Finding Your Inner Self

Paramahansa, Yogananda, *An Autobiography of a Yogi*. Los Angeles: Self-Realization Fellowship, 1975.

*Swami Muktananda, *Conversations with Swami Muktananda*. South Fallsburg: Syda Foundation, 1981.

*Patanjali, *How to Know God*. California: Vedanta Press, 1981.

*Swami Chidvilasananda, *My Lord Loves a Pure Heart*. New York: Syda Foundation, 1996.

The Dalai Lama and Howard C. Cutler, *The Art of Happiness*. New York: Riverhead Books, 1998.

Watts, Alan, *The Book—On the Taboo Against Knowing Who You Are*. New York: Collier Books, 1966.

Mindfulness

Tart, Charles T., *Living the Mindful Life*. Boston: Shambhala, 1994.

Hanh, Thich Nhat, *Peace is Every Step—The Path of Mindfulness in Everyday Life*. New York: Bantam, 1992.

Meditation

For classes on meditation, find a center near you by contacting: *www.siddhayoga.org* on the Internet.

Borysenko, Joan, *Minding the Body, Mending the Mind.* New York: Bantam, 1988.
Understanding Your Feelings

Borysenko, Joan, *Fire in the Soul.* New York: Warner Books, 1993.

Mueller, Wayne, *Legacy of the Heart—The Spiritual Advantages of a Painful Childhood.* New York: Simon and Schuster, 1992.

Estes, Clarissa Pinkola, *Women Who Run With the Wolves.* New York: Ballantine Books, 1992.

Building Healthy Relationships

Hendrix, Harville, *Getting the Love You Want—A Guide for Couples.* New York: Harper, 1989.

Gray, John, *What You Feel You Can Heal—A Guide for Enriching Relationships.* Mill Valley, California: Heart Publishing, 1984.

Mind-Body Health

Chopra, Deepak, *Perfect Health—A Complete Mind-Body Guide.* New York: Crown Publishers, 1991.

Northrup, Christiane, *Women's Bodies, Women's Wisdom.* New York: Bantam Books, 1998.

Eating in a Healthy Way
(Books include great recipe suggestions!)

Diamond, Harvey and Marilyn, *Fit For Life II—The Complete Health Program.* New York: Warner Books, 1987.

Sears, Dr. Barry, *The Zone.* New York: Regan Books, 1995.

Eating Disorders

Pipher, Mary. *Reviving Ophelia: Saving the Selves of Adolescent Girls.* New York: Ballantine, 1994.

Using Herbs To Heal

This book has many wonderful natural solutions to a wide variety of physical problems. It is for young women as well as older ones!
Weed, Susun S., *MenopausalYears: The Wise Woman Way.* New York: Ashtree Publishing, 1992.

Smith, Ed, *Therapeutic Herb Manual.* Williams, Oregon: Ed Smith. 1999. (Available at Whole Foods Market)

Death

Rinpoche, Sogyal. *The Tibetan Book of Living and Dying.* San Francisco: Harper, 1994.

Dream Interpretation

Lukeman, Alex, *What Your Dreams Can Teach You.* St. Paul, Minnesota: Llewellyn Publications, 1993.

Angels

Burnham, Sophy, *A Book of Angels.* New York: Ballantine Books, 1990.

Synchronicity

C. J. Jung, *Synchronicity: An Acausal Connecting Principle.* Princeton, New Jersey: Princeton University Press, 1972.

*These books can be ordered on-line at *www.bookstore.siddhayoga.org* or by calling 1-888-422-3334.

All other books can be ordered on-line through Barnes and Noble.com or Amazon. com.